Connemara and Elsewhere

Connemara and Elsewhere

EDITOR Jane Conroy

CONTRIBUTORS John Elder / Nicolas Fève / Tim Robinson

Connemara and Elsewhere

First published 2014
by Prism
Prism is an imprint of the
Royal Irish Academy.
19 Dawson Street
Dublin 2

www.ria.ie

ISBN 978-1-908996-37-4

British Library Cataloguing in Publication Data. A CIP catalogue record for this book is available from the British Library.

Book design and layout by Nicolas Fève

Printed in Northern Ireland by Nicholson Bass

10 9 8 7 6 5 4 3 2 1

Contributors

John Elder

From 1973 to 2010 John Elder taught English and Environmental Studies at Middlebury College, where his special interests in the classroom were American nature writing, Romantic poetry, and Japan's haiku tradition. His three most recent books – *Reading the mountains of home, The frog run* and *Pilgrimage to Vallombrosa* – each combined discussions of literature and environmental history, descriptions of the Vermont landscape and memoir. Since retirement from full-time teaching he has devoted much of his time to learning about and playing Irish traditional music.

Nicolas Fève

Nicolas Fève's photographic practice focuses on the relationship between text and image. His work has been exhibited in the William Frank Gallery, Dublin; the Galway City Museum (Tulca Festival of Visual Arts); the Clifden Arts Festival; the Franco-Irish Literary Festival at Dublin Castle and the Alliance Française, Dublin. His photographs have also been used on book covers, CD covers and by the Bibliothèque Mazarine, Paris. He first encountered Tim Robinson's work on his move to Ireland in 1998.

Tim Robinson

Tim Robinson studied mathematics at Cambridge, taught in Istanbul, worked as a visual artist in Vienna and London, and moved to the Aran Islands in 1972, where he turned to writing and cartography. His paintings and constructions have been exhibited at IMMA and the Hugh Lane gallery. His books include *Stones of Aran: Pilgrimage* and *Labyrinth*, the *Connemara* trilogy, and a suite of essays, *My time in space*.

Jane Conroy, Editor

Jane Conroy is from Connemara. Having studied in NUI Galway and Paris-IV (Sorbonne) she returned to Galway, where she is Professor Emerita of French. A member of the Royal Irish Academy, her publications include works on the cultural and literary history of early modern France, French perceptions of Ireland, and the circulation of ideas through travel. A recent collaborative work is Ireland illustrated (2014), an online database of illustrated travel accounts.

Contents

Editor's foreword — Jane Conroy / viii

Acknowledgements / xi

Introduction: unfolding the map — John Elder / 1

Browsing *Connemara*: **a photographic essay** — Nicolas Fève / 25

Elsewhere — Tim Robinson / 127

Where are the nows of yesteryear? / 129

The tower of silence / 136

Contrescarpe / 139

List of images / 143

Works cited / 146

Editor's foreword

JANE CONROY

Every book has a largely unwritten history in which authors, editors, supporters, publishers and printers play variable roles. The story of this book has been a particularly harmonious one. It began with the idea that it would be interesting to bring Tim Robinson's writing on Connemara, which is so visually evocative and sensorially rich, into contact with a graphic or photographic record of aspects of that world. Tim Robinson's openness to this prospect led to a search for the right person to create the images, and this led on to a meeting with Nicolas Fève, a dedicated reader of Tim Robinson's work, whose recent photographic exhibitions had focused on Connemara. The success of that first encounter gave shape to much of what follows in this book. There was immediate agreement that the photographs of Connemara would not be straightforward illustrations, and that the photographic essay would be a visual response to Tim Robinson's writing, placing selected passages side by side with associated images, or overlaying text on image, exploring their relationship and the capture of brief realities in different media. This purposeful wandering through the text is suggested by the essay's title, 'Browsing *Connemara*'. It forms the central part of the book.

The final section, 'Elsewhere', arose from a reading by Tim at one of the Roundstone Conversations which for many years he and Máiréad have held for the benefit of people around them who are interested in discussing and writing about place and story – another illustration of how their presence has contributed to Connemara in more than literary and cartographic ways. The three pieces which make up 'Elsewhere' mark a crucial moment in Tim Robinson's writing when, after years spent meditating on the west of Ireland, and writing about it, his mind, as he says, 'is turning elsewhere'. His agreement to have them feature as the closing section of this volume provides a landmark which will be appreciated by all who follow his writing. Many commentators and reviewers have written memorably about Tim Robinson's books on the west of Ireland, among them several members of the Atlantic Archipelagos group.

To present Tim's work, and Nicolas Fève's contribution, an ideal choice was John Elder, whose commentaries on Tim's writing had included the introduction to the New York edition of *Stones of Aran: labyrinth* (2009), and who had given a keynote lecture at the Atlantic Archipelagos' 2011 conference 'Perspectives on Tim Robinson', hosted by the Moore Institute, NUI Galway. In addition to his role as literary critic and author, John Elder shares Tim Robinson's preoccupation with environmental issues: his perceptive introduction was the final element to be put in place.

Because of Tim Robinson's importance as a topographical writer and map-maker, and because of the Robinsons' generosity as benefactors of the west of Ireland community in numerous ways, not least through providing a unique space for learning and research, and endowing the James Hardiman Library with an invaluable archive, the National University of Ireland, Galway, was glad to support the publication of this book. It is a further link in a relationship which the University values highly. The Royal Irish Academy, of which Tim Robinson is a member, was equally pleased to recognize his work by publishing the book. Its external and internal reviewers' comments have been of great value in reaching final decisions about content, as has the expertise of its publications section.

In several respects this book challenges ways of seeing and interpreting signs on paper, whether graphic or language-based. It has demanded close attention to design and typesetting. The layout has needed to be flexible, to suit both forms of expression, and exploit the possibilities of each page. This leads to particular typographic effects, such as changes in font size, to retain a visual connection between words and image, as, for example, where text on one page aligns with strands of wire on the facing page (pages 56–57) or with the horizon (pages 60–61). Elsewhere, text is overlaid on image (pages 36, 37, 91, 92), inviting a reading of the image through the lens of the text, where the text may channel the reader's interpretation of the image, or the reverse. Apart from these and other effects of positioning and typesetting, attentive readers may notice minor alterations to the original text. These occur in the photographic essay where, during discussions about this project, Tim Robinson suggested small changes to the text to suit the flow of text and image, or to clarify a quotation out of context. Passages which are not quoted verbatim are indicated by the words 'adapted from' before the title of the the source work.

Tim Robinson's work has offered many readers new ways into Connemara and into meditating on their own experience of it. This is as true for those of us who are from Connemara, as for those who live on its fringes and those who engage with it more fleetingly. He has been described by Robert Macfarlane as 'forever scrambling over boundaries, clambering over walls, literally and metaphorically', hence the wide reach of his writing and its appeal to readers of many kinds. It, together with his archive in NUI Galway, will continue to act as a stimulus for readers, writers, and researchers with a myriad of interests, ranging from cultural history and philosophy through visual art to place and identity. This book offers a further point of entry to the places and lifeworlds he evokes, exploring convergences between printed word and sensory perception, especially vision, and how these interactions affect our relationship to environment and our identity.

The intention of this book is not particularly to document Connemara in the first decades of this millennium, yet future readers will find in it a powerful sense of its shifting patterns over long periods of time, its people, their settlements and their stories, and the earth itself, recorded through the personal vision of Tim Robinson and Nicolas Fève, and the reading of these by John Elder. The final section, 'Elsewhere', which moves us away from Connemara is a reminder that there are other places of memory for Tim Robinson to explore in his own unique way.

Acknowledgements

Thanks are due to many people for their help in creating this book. The contributors and editor are especially grateful to the National University of Ireland, Galway for its generous support, and to the Royal Irish Academy for its wholehearted collaboration. Particular thanks are due to Tom Joyce of the Galway University Foundation, and to the President of NUI Galway, Dr Jim Browne, for seeing the value of the project and for their encouragement. We wish, too, to record our appreciation of the Royal Irish Academy's publications division, notably Ruth Hegarty and Roisín Jones for their suggestions and customary commitment to the highest production values.

For permission to reprint extracts from Tim Robinson's writing we are indebted to the following publishers: Penguin Books Ltd for passages from *Connemara: listening to the wind* (2007), *Connemara: a little Gaelic kingdom* (2009), and *Connemara: the last pool of darkness* (2012); Lilliput Press for passages from *Setting foot on the shores of Connemara* (1996) and *My time in space* (2001). We also thank Lilliput Press for permission to reproduce Richard Murphy's poem 'Hexagon', originally from the collection *The price of stone* (Faber 1985), reprinted in Richard Murphy, *Poems 1952–2012* (Lilliput Press 2013). The *Dublin Review of Books* is thanked for allowing us to reprint passages from 'A land without shortcuts' which appeared in its Spring 2012 issue.

Individual contributors owe debts of gratitude to friends, advisors and family, who have helped their work in a variety of ways. Not all of them can be named here, but special mention must be made of some. Foremost among these are Máiréad Robinson and Derval Conroy, whose practical assistance and many insights were invaluable throughout the entire development of the book. Encouragement and belief in the project came from many others, most notably Rita Elder, Séamus and Veronica Conroy, Michèle and Bernard Fève, and John Waddell. Warm thanks, too, go to Richard Murphy for his gift of the manuscript of 'Walking on Sunday' to Nicolas Fève, and for his kind support.

Introduction: unfolding the map

JOHN ELDER

Cartographic

Tim Robinson's *Connemara* trilogy is the culmination of a sustained effort of exploration and attentiveness that began when he and his wife Máiréad moved to the Aran Islands in 1972. Over the thirty years between their settling in Ireland and the beginning of this project, he produced five books and three maps focused on the rocky, layered realm that encompasses the Aran Islands, Connemara and the adjacent portion of County Clare known as the Burren. *Pilgrimage*, the initial volume of *Stones of Aran*, was published in 1986, while the second volume, *Labyrinth*, came out in 1995. These two remarkable books immediately assured Robinson of a permanent place on the shelf that holds the scientifically informed, speculative and at the same time highly personal narratives of such earlier masters as Gilbert White and Henry David Thoreau. In the first of them he recorded in a startlingly comprehensive way his circumambulation of the big island, Árainn (also commonly known as Inis Mór), while in its successor he related his quartering of its highly complex interior. Robinson's tenacity as an explorer and observer in these books was fully matched by the drama of his voice, in which eloquence and occasionally fervour contended with a grumbling scepticism about his own enterprise – and sometimes about the capacities of language itself.

Three shorter works of this period, *Setting foot on the shores of Connemara* (1996), *My time in space* (2001) and *Tales and imaginings* (2002), unpacked a number of the historical and personal themes incorporated into *Stones of Aran* – just as a bedrock map of the Aran Islands lays out the tectonic collisions and erosion that raised, exposed and then separated these ancient outcroppings. Indeed, mapping has been a complementary endeavour to his writing throughout Tim Robinson's career in Ireland. From his studies of Mathematics as an undergraduate at Cambridge to his latter-day fascination with the fractal theories of Benoît Mandelbrot, he has been intrigued by the geometry of irregular surfaces and boundaries. In his longer narratives, in the gazetteers accompanying his maps, and in those maps alike, he is also drawn to the dimension of time that inflects all our experiences of space.

In 1984 the Robinsons moved from the Aran Islands to Roundstone, the harbour-town of Roundstone Bay. During their first two years in this new home, while synthesizing his adventures and researches on Árainn for the first volume of *Stones of Aran,* he also completed three extraordinarily detailed maps of the mysterious hinterlands west and south of Galway. Published in 1990 by Folding Landscapes, the cartography studio and company established in Roundstone by Tim and Máiréad Robinson, *Connemara: a one-inch map, with introduction and gazetteer* expressed the vast ambition compressed within his highly localized projects as a writer and artist. Indeed, such projects accomplished at the extreme edge of Europe, and on ground still showing the grievous effects of famine and emigration, could be characterized by the same quality William Hazlitt ascribed to Wordsworth's *Lyrical ballads*—'a certain proud humility'. In his writings and his maps alike, Robinson stations himself at the edge out of a desire to rediscover the centre.

A one-inch map is drawn at the scale of one inch to a mile. This means that, in depicting a peninsula of less than forty miles in extent (even including Connemara's westernmost scatter of islands in that total) Robinson has still produced a map of over three and a half feet in width, over two and half feet in height. He began in this case, as with all three of his maps, with the superbly accurate Ordnance Survey Maps of Ireland created by the Royal Engineers starting in 1839. Though precise in the contours of the shorelines, the course of rivers and the placement of townlands, these maps were seriously deficient in two other ways when compared with Robinson's. For one thing, the military cartographers commissioned to map the British Empire's Irish possessions were not as a rule proficient in the Irish language. Their best attempts to translate or transliterate Irish placenames often missed the mark, while in other cases they either recorded later names in English or simply imposed their own English names. In such a long-settled region it would of course be difficult to speak of any placename as original. Still, the pre-Ordnance Survey names that evolved over the centuries had in fact conveyed important mythic, cultural, biological and political information for dwellers in these demanding environments.

As a Yorkshireman arriving in Connemara after pursuing his calling as an artist in Istanbul, Vienna and London, Tim Robinson soon perceived the crucial role of earlier names in shoring up communities thrown out of kilter by the subtractions and accretions of Empire. Essential to his mapping was thus a kind of cultural and linguistic ground-truthing which relied upon local guides and storytellers. He wanted to participate in the recovery of Irish names not only for the townlands and rivers of Connemara but also for certain landforms and ancient standing stones that had never been named at all on the Ordnance Survey maps. One could also turn this collaborative impulse around, as Robinson does in *The last pool of darkness*, the concluding volume of *Connemara*, when he acknowledges parenthetically that the mapping was also a vehicle for meeting his new neighbours and making himself more fully at home: '(cartography for me being mainly an excuse to enter anywhere and question anyone)'. He rarely uses the language of reparation or truth and reconciliation in his books or gazetteers, but his desire to contribute to such processes as a writer and cartographer has always been clear. The extremely high regard in which his work is held, not only by other writers and artists in Ireland and abroad but also by his strong following in the west of Ireland, reflects both the power and originality of his work and the authentic, respectful and dignified interest he takes in the corner of rural Ireland where he has sent down his own roots.

Beyond its emphasis on Irish names, Robinson's map is distinguished by the extraordinary precision with which he has drawn in the high and low ground, the high-water marks, shingles and offshore rocks exposed at low tide, the cultivated land, old woodlands, dried-up lakes and forestry land, as well as a variety of drumlins and other geological deposits. Unlike the topographical formats with which I am more familiar, Robinson's map of Connemara indicates shorelines, contours and elevations without recourse to encoded shades of green and blue. By restricting himself to fine black lines on an otherwise white map he is able to include an astounding variety of geological, historical, agricultural and linguistic information while also suggesting with all that blank space how much more remains to be added.

I have a framed copy of Tim Robinson's Connemara map on one wall of my study in Vermont. It hangs beside an old four-paned window looking into the canopy of a red-oak tree beside our house in the village of Bristol. In reading the three volumes of *Connemara* as they appeared over the space of five years, I often set down the books to walk over and peer into this map. I wanted to locate the paths Robinson had threaded and then described in writing. Gazing into the map I could envision Ireland, while looking out the window I returned to my own Vermont home. I gradually came to realize, however, that this map – horizontal to the window's vertical but similar to it in size – also illuminates certain aspects of Vermont's past and present. Ours too is a place in which nineteenth-century depopulation and social collapse set their seal on rustic loveliness now experienced as iconic by those from more crowded and prosperous places.

Artists who lavish their attention on landscapes and communities that might have seemed far from the mainstream hold open a door for kindred spirits in farflung regions. Ireland's Seamus Heaney, Derek Walcott from Saint Lucia in the West Indies and Joseph Brodsky, born in Russia, have in this regard all acknowledged their debt to Vermont's Robert Frost. Through his defiantly localized identification with the old-fashioned settlements and resurgent forests of northern New England, Frost confirmed for these poetic successors the value of their own particular settings and heritages, including neighbours' archaic utterances remembered from childhood. Similarly, Robinson's achievements have enormous value today for all of us who feel passionately affiliated with richly marginal landscapes. He offers a crucial resource for anyone seeking to assert the history and value of their homes far from the capitals.

In 1996, the year after *Pilgrimage* appeared, Folding Landscapes published *Oileáin Árann: a map of the Aran Islands, with a companion to the map*. It was followed in 1999 by *The Burren: a map of the uplands of north-west County Clare*. (Both build upon simpler versions produced while the Robinsons were still living on Aran.) The scale of these maps was even more extravagantly expansive than that of Tim Robinson's one-inch map of Connemara: two and a quarter inches to the mile for the Aran Islands map and two inches for the Burren. Such dramatic magnification was obviously facilitated by the considerably smaller areas now needing to be explored and catalogued – especially in the case of the Aran Islands. But they also anticipated a central theme in the *Connemara* trilogy to which Robinson was now turning. Namely, that the closer one looks, the larger any part of the world becomes. As he put this near the end of the volume entitled *A little Gaelic kingdom,* 'there is more space, there are more places, within a forest, among the galaxies or on a Connemara seashore, than the geometry of common sense allows.'

Connemara: listening to the wind was published in 2006, with *The last pool of darkness* appearing in 2008 and *A little Gaelic kingdom* coming out in 2011. (Tim Robinson has stipulated that *The last pool of darkness* should now be considered as the concluding volume, and *A little Gaelic kingdom* as the middle unit in the sequence.) The trilogy resembles *Stones of Aran* in important ways, foremost among them the shared impulse to weave the stories of geology, mythology, religion, history and current social and environmental challenges into a narrative framed and unified by references to local topography. Because the meaning of a place is inseparable for Robinson from the history of that place, its name too is an essential part of its significance. As he writes in *The last pool of darkness*, 'Placenames are pedlars' packs full of assorted items; only the placename itself holds them together. Time is the pedlar…'

There is also a dramatic difference of feeling and organization between the Aran and Connemara books, though. The former are marvellously and essentially compact, maintaining a clear topographic and schematic structure to which the author's speculative and associative responses are firmly tethered. Upon setting foot on Connemara, by contrast, Robinson's writing becomes more improvisatory, his relationship with his own persona both more wry and more self-revealing. He seems at first to feel that his new home on Roundstone Bay is primarily a safe harbour from which to wrap up both the second volume of *Stones of Aran* and to fill in the significant details on his two-and-a-quarter inch map of the islands. Even when his attention as a writer does decisively shift to the trilogy's first volume, *Listening to the wind*, he seems psychologically to be in Connemara but not yet of it. In a powerful passage introducing that book he describes the 'shriek of sedge bent double out on the heath, grinding of shingle sucked back by the reflux, slow chamfering of a stone's edge by blown sand grains', then goes on to say, 'Such vast, complex sounds are produced by fluid generalities impacting on intricate concrete particulars.' His remarkable gift for listening is at the same time a token of needing to take his bearings, of gathering himself before moving out into a new habitat.

In projecting where he, and his book, will go from here his language is notably deliberate. 'I am aware of the selectivity of my written responses to living in Connemara. I concentrate on just three factors whose influences permeate the structures of everyday life here: the sound of the past, the language we breathe, and our frontage on the natural world.' When he and Máiréad first fetched up in the Aran Islands that had seemed a transformative fact. As his titles for the two volumes of *Stones of Aran* reflected, it was a pilgrimage to be completed, a labyrinth to be threaded. Connemara, sundered by no sea, seems to have felt both more contingent and more continuous with his life before and after – a choice that could at any moment be reconsidered.

Robinson relates a telling story midway through this first part of *Connemara*, about a proposal (just as he is preparing to plunge into the trilogy) to build a luxury marina right outside their window in Roundstone: 'This shock almost determined us to leave Connemara – and in one way I was glad of it. After all, we had spent nearly thirty years in the west, and so perhaps it was time for another drastic change in our lives; it also appeared that I had made all the maps and written all the books I had in me about the little areas I had explored here, and that whatever I was to create in the future on the terrifying mental blank sheet that confronted me at that time, it would not relate to Ireland.' However, the development scheme in question ended up being indefinitely deferred, and just a page later Robinson returns to the question of where they will now live in quite a different mood: 'In the meantime we have become more philosophical about the proposal and less proprietorial about peace and beauty; also, I have started on the present book, finding that there is still an infinity of material on Connemara for me to chisel literature out of to my heart's content or discontent.'

Whereas in *Stones of Aran* Tim Robinson began by exploring the shoreline of Árainn and only then forged into the island's labyrinthine interior, here he begins by walking directly into the soggy heart of the peninsula, Roundstone Bog. For a writer who can often be so cagey, his irony nearly as impenetrable as the twisted heaths of a bog, Robinson can also be breathtakingly candid and boyish. Near the beginning of *Listening to the wind* he writes, 'The bog is not for me an emblem of memory, but a network of precarious traverses, of lives swallowed up and forgotten. I plan to revisit every part of it and rescue all its stories, and write them in this book.' It is not that he expects to decipher or otherwise redeem this pandemonium of natural noises and historical voices. But he will at least register the lineaments of the land and the stories of its inhabitants as fully as his own capacities allow: '"Tell only happy hours" is an exhortation carved on old sundials, but I was happy to let the plantain, with its narrow leaves like a dozen or a score of old-fashioned watch hands, tell all the island's hours at once, the bitter ones with the rest.'

Indeed, in this landscape where the Great Hunger was not an anomaly but rather 'the keystone in a triumphal arch of suffering', many of the stories Robinson reads are harrowing – as in the old potato ridges showing 'in the green turf like ribs in a famished beast'. Even when climbing Errisbeg, the highest elevation of Roundstone Bog, he encounters what feels to him like a 'self-scattering' vista of fear: 'The outline of each lake bristles with projections, every one of which is spiny; they stab at one another blindly. There is a fractal torment energizing the scene, which is even more marked in aerial photographs, in which the lakes seem to fly apart like shrapnel.' The trauma of history and the menace of impersonal and sometimes indecipherable natural process are compounded in our own day by a commercially motivated assault on 'the old, wild, weird places' and a hunger for profit that 'corrupts our eyes'.

In *A little Gaelic kingdom* and *The last pool of darkness* Robinson covers more ground than in *Listening to the wind*, both on foot and in his range of references, as he tries to find some consoling balance in this discombobulating world. In the former of these two works he traces the intricacy of Connemara's southern shore, telling the story of revolutionaries like Patrick Pearse who were drawn there, as well as tracing the struggles, survival and recovery of the peninsula's Irish-speaking regions, or Gaeltacht. It's here that his evocation of fractals from atop Errisbeg is fulfilled, and just as the saga of Pearse frames the first part of this volume the ideas of the mathematician Benoît Mandelbrot preside over its conclusion. Mandelbrot applied the word fractal (from the Latin for 'broken') in describing the replication of certain forms over many different scales. As we look more and more closely at the manifold irregularities of a coastline, for instance, we discover that they 'exhibit a degree of self-similarity over a range of scales and are therefore too complicated to be described in terms of classical geometry, which would indeed regard them as broken, confused, tangled, unworthy of the dignity of measure'.

Just as Mandelbrot's thinking about fractals informed the trilogy's second volume, the philosophy of Wittgenstein frames its third. Robinson begins his preface to it by writing, 'In 1948 Ludwig Wittgenstein fled the seductions of Cambridge, where he was the unchallenged star of the Philosophy Department, to a friend's holiday cottage in Rosroe, a fishing hamlet on a rugged peninsula separating the mouth of Killary Harbour from the bay of Little Killary. "I can only think clearly in the dark," he said, "and in Connemara I have found one of the last pools of darkness in Europe."' *The last pool of darkness* concentrates on the western reaches of the peninsula, just as its predecessor followed the southern shore. Not only was the west where Wittgenstein chose to hunker down and think, but it was also where two other remarkable episodes in Irish history played themselves out: the establishment of Marconi's research station from which the first trans-Atlantic radio signals were transmitted in 1907 and the nearby landing-place of the aviators Alcock and Brown in 1919 after their flight from Newfoundland. The problem occupying Wittgenstein as he undertook his own strategic retreat was one of which Robinson was highly aware as he too tried to manage his own landing in Connemara and to write accurately, comprehensively and unsentimentally about what he discovered there on the ground: 'the difference between seeing something and seeing it as something'.

Solas / Dolas

Tim Robinson devotes one chapter of *A little Gaelic kingdom* to a group of islands near Carna on the peninsula's southern coast. His narrative of being rowed to these formerly inhabited outposts, and of walking across the sands to some of them at low tide, is tinged with melancholy. The islands' residents had led an austere and laborious life, made yet more challenging by the hostility of colonial officials and the difficulty of arranging schooling for the children. One window after another went blank, until a day came when all their houses were empty. When Robinson visited the island of Bior Mór, or Oileán Bheara, sixty years after its last inhabitant had departed, he found only a 'settlement mapped out in fallen stone'. Such experiences were familiar during the many years he spent exploring, mapping and writing about Connemara. From Killary Harbour to Roundstone Bog, Ros Muc to Spiddal, ruins like these, along with other traces of foundered hope, proliferate in that windswept, rocky land.

Amid the collapse of walls and roofs on Bior Mór, though, Robinson discovered dozens of wild leeks which had obviously been cultivated in order to enliven the hardscrabble diets of those long-ago islanders. And when he and his companion rowed across to take their tea and sandwiches on Bior Beag, the nearby little sister of Bior Mór, he was delighted to find 'lots of tiny adder's-tongue ferns at my elbow, and fat fluffy seagull chicks tucked in by stones here and there in the tufted grass.' Loveliness persisted in the stony tumble, evoking the elemental beauty that had surely suffused those vanished communities too. Robinson quotes the last man to inhabit Bior Mór, whose words were recorded in Seán Mac Giollarnáth's book *Mo dhúthaigh fhiáin* (My wild native land): 'We didn't feel a bit of loneliness or distress, for we had the produce of earth and strand every day of the year. I had my boat to go to Mass on Sundays, for cutting seaweed and fishing and setting lobster pots. It was the boat that brought the turf in for me and took out the bags of winkles and scallops in the winter. I was the happy man out there.'

Tim Robinson concludes his chapter on these islands with a meditation on 'the ancient magic of the *so/do* (good/bad) prefixes in the Irish language. *Solas/dolas*, bright/dark; *soiléir/doiléir*, distinct/obscure; *soineann/doineann*, fair weather/stormy weather; *sólás/dólás*; solace/dolour…I could map all my island findings and feelings in such twinned opposites'. Indeed such opposites organize all three volumes of his remarkable *Connemara* project. Sympathy for vanished or attenuated rural communities reaches so deep for Robinson as to become a painful identification with their losses. By the same token, though, in imagining so fully what their lives may have been and attaching those images both to the scattered objects that remain and to the local narratives and lore that continue to grow where they first took root, his impulse of compassion can also spark an experience of powerful longing. Despite Connemara's long history of oppression, plague, famine and massacre – which Robinson characterizes in the essay 'Space, time and Connemara' as 'a river of sorrows' – the living record of 'a singular culture' abides – 'not that of the provincial gentry, but of the humble farm- and fisherfolk – a culture which conserved ancient words and ways, and had its matted and tenacious roots in a sense, deeper than any economic or legal realities, of being in its own place'.

Mandelbrot's theory of fractals has helped scientists to describe the dynamic structure within clouds, currents and other non-linear phenomena, just as it also ratifies Tim Robinson's impulse to focus on the minute and specific phenomena that lend a place its character. Intricacy is essential to the world as he perceives it, and a little section of this windswept peninsula in western Ireland expands as one begins to pace off the undulations within the larger curves of the shore: 'over a large range of scales the length of a coastline increases as if it would never stop, the closer it is investigated.' In addition, Mandelbrot's theorem ultimately provokes Robinson to a compelling insight into the enduring significance of the traditional Celtic aesthetic and world-view: 'Perhaps one could claim that fractal geometry is to Celtic art as Euclid is to classical art. While the mainstream of European culture has pursued its magnificent course, another perception has been kept in mind by the Celtic periphery…in a word, that a fascinating sort of beauty arises out of the repetitive interweaving of simple elements. The beauty of nature is often of this sort. In Connemara, which is pre-eminently the land of "dappled things" – drizzly skies, bubbly streams, tussocky hillsides – one recognizes the texture.'

Beyond the fact that the photographs of Connemara by Nicolas Fève included in this volume are so arresting and memorable in their own right, they offer a valuable context within which to explore the significance of 'dappled things' in Tim Robinson's writing. Fève juxtaposes photographs with passages from Robinson's Connemara books and maps in ways that reinforce the author's descriptions and illuminate his implications. The image entitled 'Déjà vu' is a particularly striking one. It shows a twisted black double-strand of wire angling upward to the image's left, strung above the dark grey of a dead-flat horizon and silhouetted against the lighter, swirling gray of an overcast sky. Four tufts of dark wet wool have been snagged on the old wire's barbs. The long fibres curving to the left above and below each of those tufts register a steady wind that sweeps across this sodden world.

Early on in *Listening to the wind*, Robinson recalled 'the shepherds of old times for whom the bog was a familiar workplace, who strode out vigorously and climbed boulders to scan the levels, and shouted to each other…'. That boisterous era may have passed, but wool still clings to the wire, sheep still forage for grass among the sedges and farmers still turn them out under the blustery sky and gather them back into sheltering enclosures. Robinson's world is a flicker of light and dark, clouds moving in the same direction as the blowing wool, patterns emerging from what might have seemed an undifferentiated and incomprehensible vista, then either submerging again or being left behind as the solitary walker moves on. He is in the lineage of poets like Wordsworth who help us, through their tales of haunting, to register the persistence of the absent in the play of light and shadow. It suddenly shines out, enlivening the dull backdrop.

Many of Nicolas Fève's photographs capture apparitions of this sort that are so essential to Tim Robinson's writing. As Robinson forges across the landscape, he can seem burdened by the brokenness and suffering of rural communities lashed by indifferent powers, by the challenge of organizing and conveying all that he has learned in his conversations and researches, and perhaps also by the ungovernable and fractal intricacy of his own formidable intelligence. Then he glimpses the wild leeks that seasoned the meals of a community inhabiting a blustery edge, the seagull chicks tucked into tufts of grass between the sheltering stones. Fève for his part shows us slender white horsetails growing out of their own black shadows in the rippled shallows, a single white water lily floating on a dark pond beside the elegant cleft ovals of lily pads, water-skaters riding on bubbles, between pale over-arching brambles and their thorny reflections, the sun shining at low tide out of what the poet Richard Murphy called 'a spit of wet ribbed sand'. Light slides through the landscape and the world is renewed.

All that has been scoured away in Connemara by history and the wind has opened a space for more penetrating vision, as physical and emotional exhaustion may also do. Wordsworth spoke of such instances as 'spots of time', a convergence of the spatial and the temporal so unexpected and dramatic as to hold 'a renovating virtue'. The possibility for such incandescent experience is fostered not only by the observer's hunger for significance but also by startling circumstances or relationships in the outer landscape that provoke what Wordsworth called 'visionary bleakness'. Seamus Heaney has acknowledged his own affinity, as an Irish poet, with Wordsworth, just as he has with the New Englander Frost. In introducing a collection he edited called *The essential Wordsworth*, Heaney roots that poet's achievements in 'uncanny moments' from his childhood. He writes that Wordsworth 'managed to force a way through literary convention and established modes of feeling to find in such moments not only the source of his emotional being, but the clue to his fulfilled identity'.

'Uncanny' is also the word used to translate Freud's term *das Unheimliche* (literally 'the unhomely') in *The interpretation of dreams*. It describes the mixture of familiar and unfamiliar aspects that can make a dream-image feel at once surreal and deeply meaningful. In our waking life, too, such glimpses of heightened reality can occur when common objects or events appear in a surprising setting. An artist intent upon experiencing and conveying such juxtapositions will seek a way of living and working that makes them more likely. Robert Penn Warren once said that being a poet meant 'to stand in the rain every day'. And sometimes lightning strikes. Robinson's method is to trace the incalculable complexity of Connemara's inlets and spits within the simple, if wavering, lines of his own daily outings. As he writes near the end of *A little Gaelic kingdom*, 'To make sense of it all – but no, to make sense of it would be to belittle it; let me say, to avoid total bewilderment and paralysis at its innumerable crossroads – I must follow a simple topographical trend, and thread any temporal diversions, whether into personal reminiscence or geological millennia, onto that one spatial continuity.'

Robinson's 'topographical trend' recalls that double strand of wire, a vector intersecting with the meanderings or simply the itchy backs of a world of sheep. 'Following' such a line, with its premeditated outcome, creates occasions for colliding with a tangled and unpredictable world. Such uncanny visions offer a portal through which the fractal reality of perpetual, unruly renewal can temporarily be perceived. Through them a walker, a viewer or a reader may gain access to a luminous wholeness within the dappled world. In a photogram (or botanical contact print) of bog cotton its tufted top is smeared upward in the soft focus so that it appears to be a flame above a sinuous wick. This image prepares the way for another of Fève's photographs in which a field of bog cotton blows to one side, like a collection of fluttering flames, as the last, nearly horizontal rays of the sun add their own illumination to that dense world of sedges and heaths. Such play of light across the world of bog and ocean directs a viewer's gaze to the sweep of clouds overhead in a pair of Fève's photographs depicting the 'fractals that pass…over there…over there'. In a fractal world the eye naturally flickers from heaven to earth, from earth to heaven. One of my favorite connections in this photographic portfolio (though they are separated by almost twenty pages, in fact) is between Nicolas Fève's image of mackerel skies and his close-up of one side of a grey Connemara pony, its densely dappled coat resembling a mass of clouds that swirls from withers to haunch.

Tim Robinson's capacity for singlemindedness has kept him on track in writing about and mapping western Ireland over almost four decades. An equally essential skill, however, has been his ability to detach himself at any moment from his premeditated itinerary and timetable. One crucial technique in this regard is his dead-pan humour. Such breaks from a more serious tone are effectively prepared for, in fact, by the staggeringly extensive detail into which he sometimes goes. An example of such comprehensiveness would be his sustained attention to all those offshoots of the O'Flahertys and the O'Malleys. Whenever Robinson turns his attention once again to the flamboyant genealogies of these Connemara families, a sense of incredulous delight rises in me as a reader and I never want him to stop. A similarly droll effect arises when, in *A little Gaelic kingdom*, he solemnly pauses to devote two pages to a recipe for distilling an excellent poitín. In the same vein, one of my favorite sentences in the entire trilogy comes near the end of *The last pool of darkness*: ' – and here we need to know a little of the nineteenth-century technology of flax, the basis for linen'. The word 'indefatigable' comes to mind.

There are also many occasions for more overt humour as this determined outsider investigates sites now unknown except by a few elderly inhabitants of this long-settled but severely depopulated terrain. He needs to get rescued when high tides strand him on abandoned islands, to talk himself out of trouble with enraged landowners who find him wandering where he shouldn't be – then hear his English accent. My favorite of Robinson's misadventures occurs in *A little Gaelic kingdom* when he is searching for a strange P-shaped pool along the shoreline of an island called Garomna. A boatman whom he asks responds, '"Well, […] do you see that dot? That's a sheep. It's a hundred yards beyond that sheep." But by the time I had got round the head of the harbour inlet and onto the open shore again the dot had vanished. I pressed ahead, and on rounding a bend of the shore I saw the sheep running away ahead of me. How far back had it been when it started running? I went on until I began to feel I must have gone too far. Then the sheep turned and ran back past me.' At the conclusion of this scene worthy of a Monty Python sketch, he does find the pool just as a squall is blowing in. 'I looked up, and there was that sheep sitting in the lee of a field wall just a hundred yards back along the shore, grinning at me.'

Just as revelations, mishaps and humour alike liberate Robinson from the meticulous cartography of his intentions, so too does his essential scepticism prevent him from being anchored for too long to particular revelations along the path. He is determined not to subside into satisfaction with his own terms of perception. Such determination is stated especially strongly in *The last pool of darkness*, when Robinson observes that 'Touristic pioneers of the mid nineteenth century, all following the same itinerary through Connemara – from Galway to Oughterard, Ballynahinch, Clifden, Leenaun, and so on to Westport – carried with them a set of concepts: the Picturesque, the Beautiful and the Sublime. Like a camera, or more accurately like a camera's viewfinder, this mental gadgetry enabled them to find the view: to identify what was worth looking at, to select and frame it, to record it as a verbal construction portable by memory with a view to publication. The Sublime came into play invariably as they passed through the Parish of Ballynakill…'

In his responses as a photographer both to Connemara and to Tim Robinson's writing, Nicolas Fève is alert to this tension between what we see and the expectations that govern our seeing. In a pair of images entitled 'Unfolding Roundstone', he focuses his lens through empty metal rectangles that may once have held a tourist placard or a traffic sign. In the photograph to the left he includes a stone wall, boats at anchor and a distant ridge of mountains – a composition governed by the picturesque in the foreground, by a background of mountains rising sublimely against the sky. In the other he captures two men standing beside the harbour, the nearer one holding a glass in his hand and peering quizzically back through the empty frame at the photographer. 'You looking at me?' might have been an alternative caption for this second shot. In another photograph a round, domed mirror, set up to help cars around a winding road, hangs in the sky like a distorting moon, a weird addition to what it strives to reflect. In yet another, which is paired with Richard Murphy's poem 'Hexagon', a shadowy reflection of the photographer's head and hand appears in the glass of a house's exterior window. Peering through that first layer of the image the viewer enters a room in which there is yet another window, this one looking back out into the wider world.

Anfractuous

For Tim Robinson, to walk through the world paying close attention to what he sees is also to submit to an unending process of collapse and erosion. Despite his grave, and understandable, reservations about the T.S. Eliot who produced 'Sweeney Erect', Robinson has found himself powerfully, and also understandably, attracted to one startling word in that poem. This is 'anfractuous' which 'means, according to the *OED*, sinuous or circuitous', and in that regard describes the lengthening shoreline around which his trilogy has pursued its own recursive meander. But this word, 'with the sound of fracturing in its heart', speaks to another aspect of Robinson's experience as well. As his fractal path through space also winds through time, things fall apart. Solid facts tumble into scraps and edges on the ground, then wind and water set to work again. In the face of such ceaseless reduction and transformation, 'anfractuous', he suggests, 'seems to answer not just to the winding course of the south Connemara coast but to its intimate texture, with its heaps of boulders worn into smoothly curving rims and basins by the almost ceaseless poundings of the waves'.

Where Tim Robinson's story of eleven years in the Aran Islands felt to a reader like the report from a carefully planned expedition, his initial accounts of setting foot in Connemara conveyed a less predictable experience. When he and Máiréad earlier decided to move on, 'our plan was to resettle ourselves in London, whence I would return now and again while finishing off my research towards a map of south Connemara. But before we did so I wanted to show M my new-found land, and so we came across by the little open ferryboat of those days to Ros a' Mhíl and set off to cycle around Connemara. Under September sunshine and showers the countryside was at its most seductive; M was amazed and appalled by the beauty and amplitude of the terrain I had rashly undertaken to map.' When they come upon a studio and apartment available to rent in Roundstone 'M worked it out that we should make this the base, not for the mapping of south Connemara but of the whole of Connemara; while this was in progress – which would surely only take a year or so, said I, underestimating by a factor of seven, as it turned out – she could go and earn some money as a temporary office worker in London.' This 'diversion in our lives' remains permanently connected in Robinson's memory with an image from that momentous cycling adventure: an uncompleted bridge across which they pushed their bicycles as blustery weather forced them to walk the last six miles of a day that somehow lengthened into twenty-five years.

Now it seems that Tim Robinson is once more preparing, in his writing at least, to leave Connemara. In three striking new essays included in this volume he is already ranging far from its shores – to prisons and ditches in France, into weird towers looming over urban warrens and along a reverberation set up between boyhood memories of his grandparents' village in north Wales and the lecture halls of Cambridge. Even within these apparent departures from his Irish scenes, though, continuities remain. In the shingle visible through shallow water as a small boat oars away from Connemara's intricate shore, one may glimpse the same bedrock that shoulders up through Roundstone Bog.

'Contrescarpe' adopts the title of a 1974 memoir by Julien Sarrazin that takes its own name from that of a square in Paris – which echoes in its turn a term from medieval fortification fully as odd and evocative as 'anfractuous'. An Irish friend who is an archaeologist explained to Robinson that 'the inner wall of a defensive ditch is the *escarpe* and the outer one the *contrescarpe*'. When a large ditch is dug around the protective walls of a city or a castle the resulting 'spoils' are heaped up as obstructive rubble around the outside of the ditch. Such a stepwise, fractal etymology for his essay's title recalls Robinson's strategy of 'intrication' as he delved into, heaped up and ramified the majestic inwardness of Connemara. The image of fortification also expresses the fierce embrace at the heart of Sarrazin's memoir. That book arose from the death at 29 of his love, Albertine. He in his autobiography, as she had done in her 1965 autobiographical novel *L'Astragale,* recounted how amid their circumstances of poverty, crime and relentless defiance of social norms they found a 'precious and savage reason' for living in one another. Robinson's tangy evocation of a recent stay near Place de la Contrescarpe reveals once more how the name of a place (or of a *place*) can serve as his vehicle for a voyage through time. As was so often true for him in Connemara, the story embedded in a placename can serve as an opening to sympathy with the sufferings and triumphs of lives that might initially have seemed remote.

'Contrescarpe' also amplifies another aspect of Robinson's writing that I have always prized. In his wry and dignified persona he generally alludes only in passing to the passions that underlie his outlook on life. An example of such literary pointillism would be his many brief references to Proust, eventually allowing a reader to understand how much these books have meant to him as a writer without ever devoting an extended passage to *À la recherche du temps perdu*. An even more striking aspect of the trilogy (as it is of *Stones of Aran*) is the emergence within his narratives of an extended love-letter to Máiréad – whom he generally refers to in his writings simply as M. Early on he makes it clear that, though they are partners in life, he can only tell his side of the story. That fact notwithstanding, again and again her perspectives, and her ratification or redirection of his insights, are essential to his choices – as in the crucial matter of their remaining in Connemara for twenty-five years just when it seemed they were about to decamp for London.

If imagination and mathematics are two of the ways in which people can travel through time and into other lives, even while restricted to one locale, an equally powerful vehicle is the experience of love. In *The last pool of darkness*, while 'roaming the photon-drenched spaces of Roundstone Bog', Robinson begins to reflect caustically about the road that has led from Marconi's early radio station at Derrigimlagh to 'the bath of invisible communications we are all immersed in today'. But then he suddenly felt 'like sending a love-note to M back at home' with the aid of his cellphone, and was able in unjaundiced wonder to experience 'the way the complex numbers dance together, the photons flit, the electrons run and the world folds like a map for one point to kiss another'.

'Where are the nows of yesteryear?', the longest essay of these three traveller's reports posted back to Connemara, is yet another echo of Robinson's longing to accompany Proust on the search for lost time. His childhood memory of an ancient set of playthings called 'spillikins', kept at his grandparents' house in the wonderfully named town of Mold, enters into conversation with a Cambridge philosopher's perspective on time. He describes Professor Mellor's assertion that 'Our subjective experience of the flow of time…is no evidence that time really does flow; what we actually experience is change in ourselves, the accumulation of memories, of memories of memories.' It might seem to one who has just finished re-reading *The last pool of darkness*, especially with Wordsworth's spots of time in mind, that such accumulation is *how* time flows, and where it pools – which is to say, in us.

Those childhood spillikins, existing now only in Robinson's mind, remain gauges for time's inward flow. They were thin 'stems' of ivory, about five inches long and with a little emblem representing 'a Chinese sage, a sickle moon, a long-tailed bird or some fabulous species of animal' crowning one end. At the game's beginning they were dumped from the box into a pile on the floor or onto a table top, like a heap of rubble shovelled up from a fortifying ditch. After that, a player's task was to lever them out one at a time, so carefully that none of the other spillikins trembled at its departure. This remembered process is for Robinson like the task of extricating valuable 'nows' from the thickets of personal experience and regional history alike. A similar 'connoisseurship of memory', he writes, 'is the human role in this indiscriminately memorious world'.

Reading 'The tower of silence', shortest and most compressed of these three recent dispatches, feels in its global frame of reference like turning the last page of the *Connemara* trilogy and closing its final volume. When Robinson wanders into a London house that is awaiting demolition, lured by the promise of books left behind by a mysterious squatter, he discovers that the floors and attics have all been removed, leaving a vast dreamspace. 'One wall of the great empty tower had a door in it at each level, all hanging open; another wall had four tiled fireplaces one high above another.' In an uncanny realization, reminiscent of Borges, he suddenly knows that he had seen this same tower, often associated with misery and grief, in many other stations of his travels, including Istanbul, Paris, Calcutta, Bangkok and, most exotic of all, Terre Haute. Within such a thicket of associations he can make out one city within another; one moment, one life, within another. At this giddy, centrifugal moment, though, when the map of Connemara seems to have been completed, or at least abandoned, the practice of mapping still continues.

Yet another notable word to which Tim Robinson was drawn in writing the trilogy is 'superincumbent'. This term, originally drawn from botany, describes how certain flowers of his beloved heath family bend over to lean against their own fuzzy stems. The more generalized dictionary definition of 'superincumbent' he cites is of 'lying or resting and usually exerting pressure on something else'. It's a good way to express what it means to arrive in a mysterious stony land and to venture into the tenacious community that survives there after one has grown up elsewhere and pursued a wandering life. What it means, as well, to read the ground with a mind full of poetry, philosophy and mathematics. Inevitably, we superimpose what we arrive with onto what we find, and exert distorting pressure on this new world with the movement of our bodies and our minds. But a traveller may nonetheless choose to settle down into this strange new realm, juxtaposed intimately with it by the circling storms and seasons that embrace them both. If a day does come for departure, one might choose to view it as the 'twinned opposite', and in that sense the fulfillment, of the newcomer's long-ago arrival.

Such a movement beyond may feel like a *release* for one fearful of sentimentality, through forgetting the distinction between what we see and what we see things *as*. Like so many forms of release, it can at the same time be an experience of grief, a relinquishment of the inadvertent but beloved conditions of one's life. Perhaps such mixed feelings had something to do with Tim Robinson's decision to declare that *A little Gaelic kingdom*, his final volume when it was published in 2011, should actually be considered the middle unit of his trilogy. Having surrendered himself in it to the fringing intricacy of Connemara's southern shoreline he came to realize that there was never going to be a place to stop, since 'Every tale entails the tale of its own making, generalities breed exceptions as soon as they are stated, and all footnotes call for footnoting to the end of the world.' By sliding this final volume back into the middle he tucked the trilogy's fringe back underneath. It was a process of literary subduction, analogous to the submergence of one tectonic plate when meeting another plate's counter-momentum. New headlands and ridges will rise above such a zone where one geological realm has been relinquished while leaving its constituent elements available for what comes next.

With all their concreteness, precision and richness of perception, Tim Robinson's books and maps from Connemara were always about transience. They delineated traces left in the heart by the arisings and vanishings of beauty. Even in the initial sentence of his first essay about this peninsula, the 1990 'Space, time and Connemara', he was already saying goodbye: 'Connemara – the name drifts across the mind like cloud shadows on a mountainside, or expands and fades like circles on a lake after a trout has risen.'

Wool gathering

Browsing *Connemara*: a photographic essay

Nicolas Fève

Photographer's Note

NICOLAS FÈVE

The aim of the photographic essay that follows is to provide a visual exploration of the key concepts underpinning Tim Robinson's work as cartographer and writer. In proposing a visual reading of his Connemara, inspired by browsing both the trilogy and the landscape, the following essay sets out to juxtapose text and image in such a way as to heighten readers' awareness of what Tim calls 'geophany' – the visible manifestation of the earth. These photographs do not aim to illustrate specific places, but rather to reflect the hallmarks of Tim's approach.

To do this, 'Browsing *Connemara*' takes the form of a photographic essay, based on an anthology of extracts from Tim's writings, focusing in particular on the methods and practices he adopts to describe and negotiate the landscape. Three areas of exploration are central to Tim's approach, namely 'the sound of the past, the language we breathe, and our frontage onto the natural world' (*Listening to the wind*, 3). From these three areas, three specific concepts emerge which can be seen to transform a location into a place, namely beauty, strangeness and antiquity. In that transformation, in the creation of place which is the hallmark of Tim's work, a number of well-defined disciplines are exploited: cartography, folklore, toponymy, botany, urban planning, agriculture, geology. But the actual creative process of his writing of the landscape, through both maps and prose, hinges on the exploration of a number of more abstract concepts: the notion of fractality; the accumulation of detail; the importance of the step, of walking the land; the invention and re-invention of the landscape; the notion of listening and relating, both in the sense of recounting and of bringing together.

Photography, as practiced here, can be seen to hinge on these very concepts, in the way the landscape is exposed. The photographer shares with the cartographer the necessity of being on site, of walking the land. Each frame, each photograph can be read as a fragment of the greater landscape, and photography as a type of fractalization. Photography hinges on an accumulation of detail, an accumulation of points of view. Like cartography and archaeology, it is always retrospective, inventing and re-inventing a landscape which is always *déjà vu*, *déjà lu*, already seen, already read. Like toponymy, photography re-marks an element of the landscape, re-composing it. It involves what Tim defines as the science of distemics, namely 'the study of topographical sensations' laid out on paper, a type of 'phenomenology of far-off things' (*Gaelic kingdom*, 54). This photographic praxis hinges on a notion which is key to Tim's conceptualization of antiquity, namely 'the idea that the eye itself has its religion' (*Setting foot*, 208).

In concrete terms, these concepts translate themselves by an approach which plays with format and page layout, setting and framing, black and white, perspective and flattening. Oscillating between detail and panorama, between local and cosmic, as Tim's work does, the juxtaposition of text and image aims to unsettle the reader and reveal the strangeness of place.

For anyone walking the land and bringing back images of it, their activity is marked by serendipity. It is this that makes the photographer an accidental author. Photography can be understood as a wandering, a pedestrian rhetoric. Thus, photography can be understood as a practice of space, a practice of contact, with photographs as the meeting point (see, for example, p. 118–9). Thus, photography encapsulates a poetics of elsewhere and of otherness. Thus, photography creates unknown and unseen things. Thus, photography is a space of apparition, an elliptic and metonymic process of allusion and elision. Thus, photography is an art of distance. It is 'geophatic'.

To take a photograph is to define an alignment as it works for the human eye: an alignment of eye–lens–land in the instant of shooting, where the photographer is the ghost, of eye–print–seen in the instant of viewing, where the viewer is the ghost. In this respect, the photograph is an inhabited space to be looked through (see, for example, p. 109). What takes place in photography is that the photographer has to take (a) place. Lost in the surrounding 'chaosmos', photography is a means of orientation, like a geographic sundial. A shadow at such-and-such a time will tell you not where you are, but in which direction you are looking; it will tell you that 'now here' is the only starting-point from where you can see, the only starting-point that can be envisaged. How then can one consider the ever unreachable, unstable, 'unpositionable' horizon? Paul-Armand Gette raises the question in his work about limits and corresponding notions (the boundary, the ecotone, the origin), and the opening image here ('0m.') is an allusion to his ideas. The camera, opening its shutter, just for an instant, answers the question by cutting, thus deploying a modifier function. It frames and delimits an 'out-of-field'. An echo effect is engendered, giving way to a string of anamorphoses, to a variable geometry of time and space.

That echoing effect is key in representation. What is represented is always distant. The photograph re-presents the absent, retrospectively and forwardly, like an echo (the *imago vocis* in Latin). It echoes or quotes what was seen. Thus, the photograph acts like a rebus (see, for example, p. 88), like a visual and/or verbal pun, re-affirming, as does a placename in a landscape. There is a mute function of photography which invites invention, a function to which an 'I' can relate and which an 'I' can recount. By invention, *inventio*, two things can be understood here: both what ones finds and uncovers, and, as a practice, a quality of attention to a place. This invention can only happen via a poetics of vacation and vacancy (as suggested on p. 79). Hence, photographs can be seen as a place of pensiveness. The photograph is unquiet in its process of displacement, of lay-out. In this photographic translation of the land, I try to work out how the page – the invention of the page, the idea of the page, the format of the page, the use of the page and so on – underlies (under-lies) our perception of what we call a landscape, and, in return, what place is made for us and for nature.

If many of these photographs are flat, it is because they aim to highlight the quality of flatness or platitude. Firstly because, of course, they lie flat on a page, and here printers have to be thanked for their work. Secondly, because travelling through Connemara, one is often faced with a landscape with little perspective, with the Twelve Bens and the Atlantic dominating the panoramic vista. The landscape reveals itself in different layers and shades, layers of vertical plane surfaces, of standing layers, we might say (as suggested on p. 40). Nonetheless, Connemara can be tricky for a photographer to capture, because it reveals itself most in two extreme lights: a particularly diffuse light that extends as an immense grey flatness with no shadows, or a blank dazzlement, whereby the landscape can only be grasped in the light of detail (see, for example, p. 113). Thirdly, these photographs play with the quality of flatness since there is frequently a lack of classical visual perspective (see, for example, p. 117). There is no one place assigned to the viewer; hence she/he has to exercise her/his freedom, has to instigate a movement. Perspective is avoided, to the point where the eye is no longer pre-occupied.

Since photography is about unsettling and displacement, beyond is the next step, the next image, the next sentence, the next movement. In this photo-essay the act of turning the pages back and forth, encouraged by the deliberate interplay between texts and images, the explicit cross-referencing, in addition to the (at times) unsettling nature of the typography, aims to recreate the difficulty of walking the Connemara landscape. Photography here is about opening a gap, an in-between, a distance where one can find where one stands (as happens on p. 111). It transports to an estranged place. This transposition involves a poetics of the imaginary, a poetics of origin, hence what we might call a poetics of the originary. But the photograph is also a place to recuperate: to reuse, to recycle, to recover, to invent ourselves via a journey through the wording and the images of the land that is showing forth (Tim's 'geophany'). We walk on placenames, on names, on words and by moving, by taking a step aside or beyond, we weave them together and write the landscape. This browsing of *Connemara* tries to understand how writing and light travel. This 'geophatic-graphy' and epiphany, through the play of light, calls for 'geophany' to take place.

Abbreviations

Mapping south Connemara	*Mapping south Connemara*
Map	*Connemara: a one-inch map, with introduction and gazetteer*
Setting foot	*Setting foot on the shores of Connemara*
My time in space	*My time in space*
Listening to the wind	*Connemara: listening to the wind*
Last pool	*Connemara: the last pool of darkness*
Gaelic kingdom	*Connemara: a little Gaelic kingdom*
'Land without shortcuts'	'A land without shortcuts: in defence of the distinctiveness of places'

The path led me to an antique sundial inscribed with the terse motto 'Look' (which I am tempted to borrow as an epigraph for this book). Adapted from *Listening to the wind*, 391

All around the coast, a fiction, the high-water mark, posed a similar problem; rather than indicate it by a line I relived with my pen the hourly give-and-take of land and sea. *Setting foot,* 15

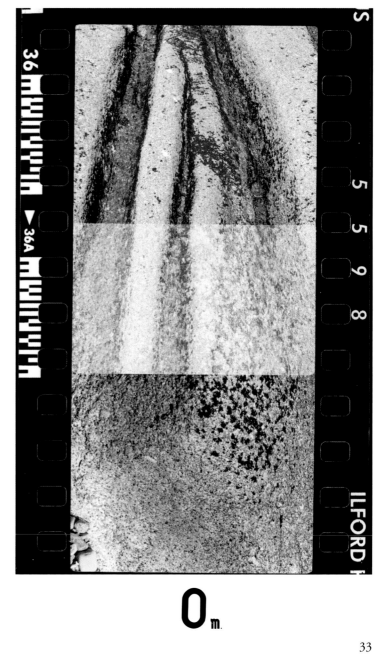

0 m.

Most Connemara skies are steeped in a decoction of tones wrung out of rainbows, but this blue had been filtered through infinities of depth to perfect purity; in fact I don't believe I'd ever seen blue of such intensity. Colour is a modality we don't need – old films and photographs show that we can get along with greys – and perhaps don't deserve, I thought. It is a gift, an ornamentation; it is the song of matter, delivered in the 'old way', ever new. *Gaelic kingdom*, 129

A preface represents the moment of writing, a fictive moment in which the book is declared complete, or abandoned as incompletable within the limits of time and talent available, and is delivered to that longed-for response, the moment of reading, which stands in the same labyrinthine relation to hearing as writing does to speech. The moment of writing, outcome of the potentially endless reshapings of sense and intricate adjustments of word to context that true writing allows and indeed consists in, is a fractal construction out of all the subsidiary moments in which words, phrases, paragraphs, chapters, have been completed. *Listening to the wind*, 3

My rule is, when I find that I am falling into repetition, to take it as a challenge to rethink, to invent the unsaid…True writing, art in general, is essentially concerned with what is yet to be defined, what may become defined through its exercise but then is to be left behind in the advance into the unknown. *My time in space*, 196

Déjà vu

How can writing, writing about a place, hope to recuperate its centuries of lost speech? A writing may aspire to be rich enough in reverberatory internal connections to house the sound of the past as well as echoes of immediate experience, but it is also intensely interested in its own structure, which it must preserve from the overwhelming multiplicity of reality. I am aware of the selectivity of my written response to living in Connemara. I concentrate on just three factors whose influences permeate the structures of everyday life here: the sound of the past, the language we breathe, and our frontage onto the natural world. I don't propose these as philosophical categories, merely use them as organizing principles, interplaying with the general topographical drive of the work. *Listening to the wind, 3–4*

Pearse's cottage

Touristic pioneers of the mid nineteenth century, all following the same itinerary through Connemara…carried with them a set of concepts: the Picturesque, the Beautiful and the Sublime. Like a camera, or more accurately like a camera's viewfinder, this mental gadgetry enabled them to find the view: to identify what was worth looking at, to select and frame it, to record it as a verbal construction portable by memory with a view to publication. *Last pool, 72*

Connemara – the name drifts across the mind like cloud shadows on a mountainside *Setting foot, 53*

Phototaxis

Unfolding

Roundstone

There is always an imaginary all-seeing eye in the head of an isolated hill, such is the persuasiveness of the topography; one feels the urge to climb it and look out from it in all directions, and if the urge is so strong it must drive others too; therefore there is someone up there at this moment looking down at us in the plain below. *Gaelic kingdom*, 58

Cities were invented to protect us from the terrors and temptations of horizons. Façades stare down the would-be-wandering eye, direct it along perspectives that terminate in monuments to the centrality of the places they occupy. *My time in space*, 14

To the artist it is intolerable that one cannot climb to one's own horizon and look beyond. *My time in space*, 72

Mám Éan / the pass of birds

As for myself, I have become a minor object of touristic interest, perhaps the only one not marked on the map. *Setting foot, 16*

Now in the act of drawing my aim was to achieve the same intimacy of physical contact with the emergent image as I had reached with the reality. – But all this is to formalize in retrospect a practice that was tentative and instinctual, and indeed to fill up with ideals the blanks on the resultant map. *Setting foot, 15*

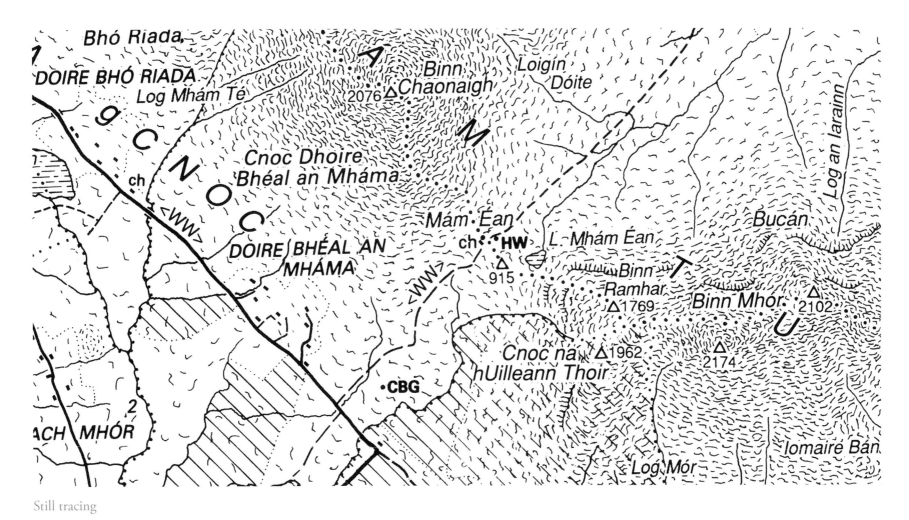

Still tracing

The top of a pass is a strange specialization of nowhere, like a crossroads; it is nothing in itself
but choice of ways and the possibility of going astray. The route from valley to valley, briefly ascending out of the
everyday life, drawing breath for a moment and then descending into it again, crosses another route that goes
from peak to peak, clambering down dangerous slopes, striding out on an easy stretch, and mounting again into extremity.
Around the saddle-point itself the lie of the land may be quite ambivalent; if visibility is limited there may be no clues from
the trends of slopes as to which is the right way. Geometrically it is a point of zero curvature, where the curvature
of the mountain route is cancelled out by the opposite curvature of the home route. Dynamically it is a point of unstable
equilibrium; on a surface of this form, a ball could rest here but the slightest disturbance will send it rolling down one way or
the other. Emblematically it is the destabilization of Stifter's tale and the certainties it propounds. (If these observations amount
to a deconstruction of the story, they are not intended as an exercise in a criticism that prides itself on being deeper than its subject,
but rather as exemplifying the fact that all true writing undermines itself, is deeper than itself. Were it not so, why would we attempt such writing?
For we already know what we know, and hope always for more.) *My time in space*, 112–113

FIGURE IN A MAP

The 'topographical sensations' arising, for instance, from crossing a pass, completing the circuit of an island, or walking out to an island accessible at low water, are privileged moments of spatial awareness, able to bear the heavy vestments of symbolism. The exhilaration of crossing one valley to another through a pass comes partly from such a journey's being a metaphor for threshold moments in which successive life-stages are simultaneously graspable, and past and present support the moment like two giant stilts. But the ground of this feeling is the geometrical configuration of the saddle-point, combining the highest and the lowest into a highly defined point of unstable equilibrium, so that you, here, are highly defined as a figure in a landscape.

The landscape itself focuses on you, pinpointing a precise 'sense of place'. Such eruptions of the meaningful into the plains of geometrical existence are themselves distractions from the quotidian inevitability of emplacement, the humble submission to the laws of perspective. It is fitting that, on a map, such singularities and discontinuities of topography as mountain summits, coastlines and passes occupy an area tending to zero with increasing fineness of drawing. *Setting foot*, 105–106   A *mám* is the amount one can scoop up between two hands, and, seen from the valley, the skyline here looks as if Beola or some such giant being had taken such a scoop out of it, as it does in many high mountain gaps of similar names. *Listening to the wind*, 369

'usque ad ultimum terrae, ubi nunc paruitas mea esse uidetur inter alienigenas', *Confessio* 1, Saint Patrick

To climb to a pass is also to leave the lowland of wordly concerns behind, but without going all the way over or choosing between the peaks to left and right of the way. This topography of doubt, of judgement or decision suspended, lends itself to my purposes in this final chapter; in short, it suits my book.

Listening to the wind, 400

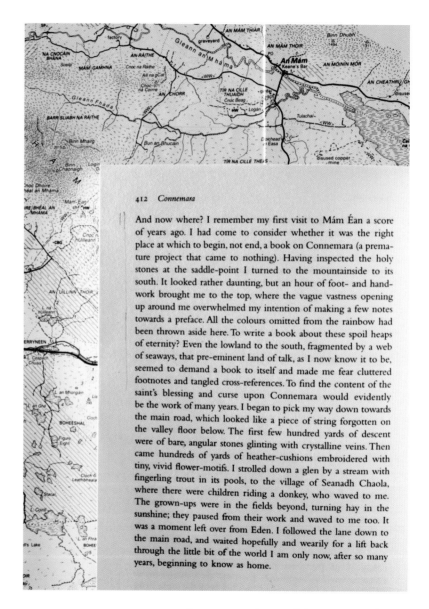

Listening to the wind, last page, and *Map*

Out of field, Na Siáin / the fairy hills

Later I was to discover that this tale of three dimensions is entirely inadequate, not just to the subjective dimensions, the ones that pass through the heart of the cartographer, but even to the objective reality of landscape. *Setting foot*, 78

That supreme space-shaper, the commanding force orthogonal to all the tentative, laterally spreading, webs of my mapwork, is immanent in much of what I have drawn or written. *My time in space*, 6

Also, since I dislike making appointments, my method of rambling along and greeting people on the road or on the shore, or calling in at cottages or indeed factories and hotels, as and when I reached them, suited me, and although it was not always efficient in terms of information-gathering, it put the people in their context.…So my map of Connemara is the record of a long walk, an intricate, knotted, itinerary that visits every place within its territory. *Setting foot, 80–81*

That the human mind can learn so much of what happened sixty or more times as long ago as the birth of the human race is wonderful; it is as if the mite no bigger than a full stop one notices running across the page one is reading could itself read that page. Plate tectonics and mantle convection have been with us long enough as a scientific theory for us to take it into our minds as a feature of our world-picture, the backdrop of the indubitable against which other claimants to our belief parade their persuasions. And if we know in our hearts that mountains and oceans have their day then our proprietorial attitude to patches of land appears in perspective, as a littleness. *Last pool, 313*

Folding landscape

46

But geology calls for overviews and is better left for hilltop consideration; in fact any hill suggests a progression from close-up observations of what is immediately under the climber's hands and feet, through rests for breath-catching and retrospection and glances ahead at intermediate delusive skylines that hide the ultimate goal, to the triumphal horizon-sweeping outlook from the summit and the crushing realization of the depths of time that weigh on a mountain top and even on the mere 987 feet of Errisbeg. *Listening to the wind*, 66

A general could plan strategies of advance and encirclement from up here; I could plan a book, and from this height it looks as if it would be achievable, all the sticking points of that contentious, foot dragging, ankle-twisting subject matter being ironed out by distance. *Listening to the wind*, 368

Enquiring out placenames, mapping, has become for me not a way of making a living or making a career, but of making a life; a mode of dwelling in a place. In composing each of the placenames instances I have given you into a brief epiphany, a showing forth of the nature of a place, I am suggesting that what is hidden from us is not something rare and occult, or even augustly sacred, but, too often, the Earth we stand on. I present to you a new word: 'geophany'. A theophany is the showing forth, the manifestation, of God, or of a god; geophany therefore must be the showing forth of the Earth. In the west of Ireland there is a language and a placelore uniquely fitted to the geophany of that land, with its skies full of migrating alphabets, waves that conspire to lift the currach ashore, its mountains like teeming udders, its foot-chilling bogs, the donkey's bray of its history, its ancient words piled on hilltops. My work is possible thanks to what I have grasped of the geophanic language of Ireland. My work thanks that language. *Setting foot*, 164

From the various hilltops I climbed to get a conspectus of the country the inner recesses of these bays looked like the roots of a marvellous silver tree. Adapted from *Setting foot*, 20

Forest tree, 4014 B.C., next page

47

I am free to concentrate on that mysterious and neglected fourth dimension of cartography which extends deep into the self of the cartographer. My task is to establish a net-

work of lines involving this dimension, along which the landscape can enter my mind, unfragmented and undistorted *Setting foot*, 20   Photogenic drawing

Accumulating impressions in a diary, I became a writer; and then, noting placenames and routes and locations on paper, a cartographer.

Perhaps it is only in hindsight that I can justify my choices of technique in such terms. Nevertheless it does strike me now that these black-on-white maps, in which shingle banks and beaches and bogs and crags and lake water and mountain heights are all represented through thousands of dots and dashes and twiddles and twirls, are elaborate disclaimers of exhaustiveness. Everywhere are these minute particulars of ink, mimicking the rough, the grainy, the oozy or the dazzling, the sensuous modalities of walking the Earth's surface; while, equally everywhere, the white, the abyss of the undiscovered, shows through. Also, it occurs to me that there is at least a coherence between this style of drawing and a cluster of images that surface everywhere in my writing, centering on the human pace, the step taken.... Though I have probably taken more steps about and on my three western marches than most of their born inhabitants, I have not put down roots in any of them. Roots are tethers, and too prone to suck up the rot of buried histories. I prefer the step – indefinitely repeatable and variable – as a metaphor of one's relationship to a place.... This controlling imagery is not entirely something I have freely chosen to elaborate, and it could become a knot-garden I have to cut my way out of. Perhaps I do need to quit these worn ways and trodden shores, to test these ideas elsewhere, to travel in search of that impossibility, the view from the horizon. *Setting foot*, 212

Quay at the beach of the women

more Point

Trá na mBan
quay
Ceártaí

Quay at the beach of the women

A range of paradoxes appears on the horizon; poetic answers to logical questions, the rational solution of problems the posing of which is an irrational act. My preferred territory lies between aesthetics and logic. *My time in space*, 62

And I used to hope that the intensity of my physical experience of Connemara would burn through all these layers of methodological tracing-paper into the final drawing, making it not just a factual record, but an expression of a feeling or a lot of contradictory feelings about the place. Perhaps if I vividly remembered walking along a certain shinglebank, I would be able to put some echo of my footsteps into the dots representing it on my map. *Setting foot*, 80

When it came to drawing my first maps, I restricted myself to black, and to linear techniques, the better to represent the interweaving of various aspects of the territory. *Setting foot*, 76

These images I am offering you – the wild-goose chase of the alphabet in the sky, the waves whispering to each other under the curragh, the donkey uttering *seanchas* from the well – are little myths, to tempt you to hear the language as if it were spoken by the landscape. *Setting foot*, 153

The   re is
        per   haps
            a tiny   curragh
                with   an out
                    board   engine
                        unzip ping
                        the still
                        ness
                        of
                        the
                        wat
                        ers.

This mysterious personage, the Fairhaired Merchant (an Ceannaí Fionn), figures in the folklore of the west of Ireland, according to which he and a companion once set off by boat to discover *bun na spéire*, the foot of the sky, as the horizon is called in Irish. *Listening to the wind*, 124–125

All horizons had been dissolved by rain. Middle distances were grey on grey; lakes lay like deflated clouds on the blurry levels. *My time in space*, 180

Derryclare Island

So, I am particularly interested in or excited by the points at which the thread of my explorations crosses itself, as it were, from various

directions, and can be knotted firmly, that is, memorably, in a way that elevates a mere location to the status of a place. *Setting foot*, 100

Blotched

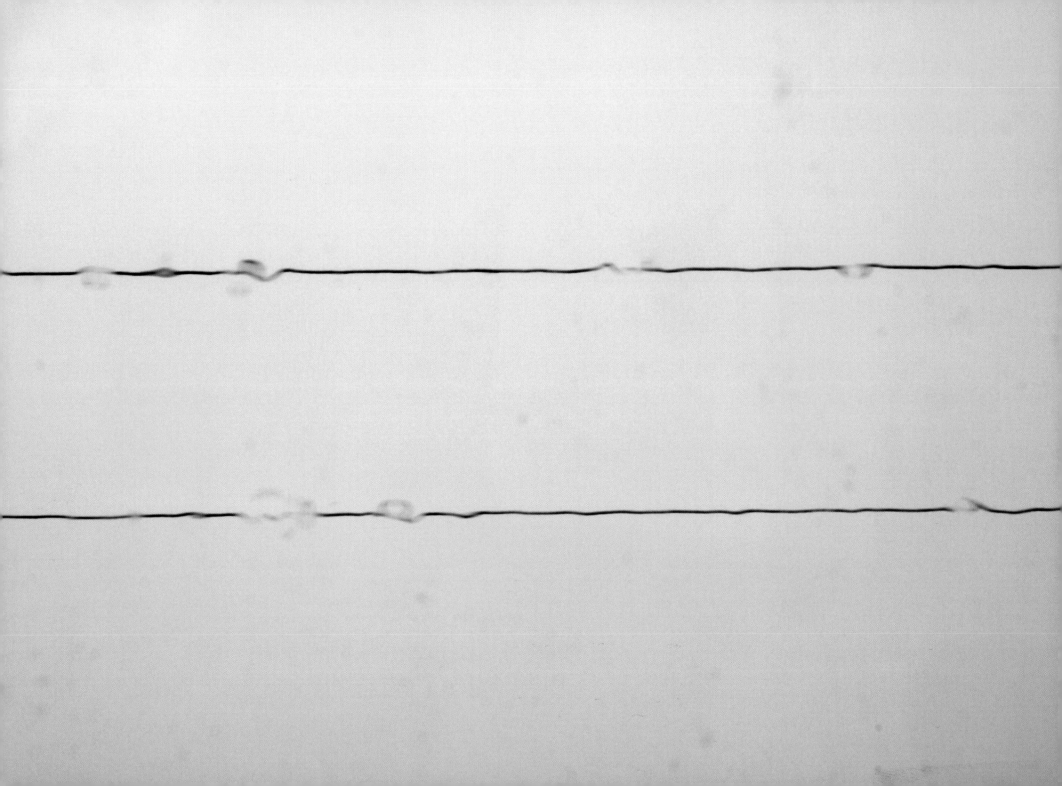

Erosion   While walking this land, I am the pen on the paper; while drawing this map, my pen is myself walking the land. The purpose of this

identification was to short circuit the polarities of objectivity and subjectivity, and help me keep faith with reality. *Setting foot,* 77

Trá na nÉan

Horizons are the eye's best attempts upon infinity; we scan them avidly as if desperate to see as far as possible or searching for escape through the threadlike gap between the impenetrable globe and the indefinite depths of the sky. *My time in space*, 11

Faul / the fences

We are spatial entities – which is even more basic than being material entities, subject to the laws of gravity. The barest of bones of the relationship between an individual and the world are geometrical; on the landscape scale, topographical. Our physical existence is at all times wrapped in the web of directions and distances that constitutes our space. Space, inescapable and all-sustaining Space, is our unrecognized god. *Setting foot, 104–105*

Perhaps the duty of consciousness in this regard is to be open to a maximal realization, a delicate and precise awareness of one's spatial relationships to the world. (Try it when watching branches swaying in the breeze, one behind another.) But this awareness, if it becomes strained and muddled, soon subsides into the indiscriminate welter of 'being at one with Nature'. Like love, it flourishes best on the very edge of loss of identity, of merging with the object; it is a dangerous leaning-over the brink of the blissfully all-dissolving Oceanic, or of the seasick existential shudders. A cliff-edge experience. *Setting foot, 10*

The cliff-edge is the controlling emblem of my life. *My time in space, 4*

Nymphaea alba

62

We could not use or even bear to look at a map that was not mostly blank. This emptiness is to be filled in with our own imagined presence, for a map is the representation, simultaneously, of a range of possible spatial relations between the map-user and a part of the world. The compass rose represents the self in these potential relationships; it is usually discreetly located in some unoccupied corner, but is conceptually transplantable to any point of the map sheet. Its meagre petals are a conventional selection of the transfinity of directions radiating from the self to the terrain. It is a skeletal flower, befitting our starved spatial consciousness. *Setting foot*, 106

Last pool of darkness

In 1948 Ludwig Wittgenstein fled the seductions of Cambridge, where he was the unchallenged star of the Philosophy Department, to a friend's holiday cottage in Rosroe, a fishing hamlet on a rugged peninsula separating the mouth of Killary Harbour from the bay of Little Killary. 'I can only think clearly in the dark,' he said, 'and in Connemara I have found one of the last pools of darkness in Europe.' His thought, a mental ascesis that matched his frugal and solitary existence there, was directed to an end, or rather to its own end. As he had written, 'The real discovery is the one that makes me capable of stopping doing philosophy when I want to. The one that gives philosophy peace, so that it is no longer tormented by questions which bring itself into question.' The particular question preoccupying him at this time concerned the difference between seeing something, and seeing it as something. For instance, his farming neighbours see this strange figure in their landscape, and see him as a madman. …The temptation, he writes, is to say 'I see it like this', pointing at the same thing for 'it' and 'this'. Hence arises a philosophical pseudo-problem. But by analyzing how we use language in such cases, we can 'get rid of the idea of the private object'. His neighbours, though, know a duck-rabbit when they see one, and forbid him to cross their land lest he frighten the sheep. Wittgenstein also lifts his eyes to the forbidden hills in search of examples of change-of-aspect:

'The concept of 'seeing' makes a tangled impression. Well, it is tangled… I look at the landscape, my gaze ranges over it, I see all sorts of distinct and indistinct movements; this impresses itself sharply on me, that is quite hazy. After all, how completely ragged what we see can appear! And now look at all that can be meant by 'description of what can be seen'.'

'*Wie gänzlich zerrissen uns doch erscheinen kann, was wir sehen!*' – what rippings and tearings in that '*zerrissen*'! And this landscape has indeed been torn. *Last pool*, 1–2

Wittgenstein himself wrote that the nature of his new investigations 'compels us to travel over a wide field of thought criss-cross in every direction' and he described his book as 'a number of sketches of landscapes made in the course of these long and involved journeyings'. The work also involved severe self-criticism: looking back at the *Tractatus* he noted, 'I have been forced to recognise grave mistakes in what I wrote.' Many of his most basic assumptions were now subjected to a shattering re-examination and thrown aside. In particular the idea that propositions describe facts as pictures show their subjects is abandoned; there are many modes of description and many sorts of proposition other than descriptions, and the meaning of a proposition is not a corresponding reality but the role the proposition plays in a particular linguistic situation, to be elucidated by the most subtle and painstaking observation of its behaviour in the stream of life. *Last pool*, 35

'One keeps stumbling and falling…and the only thing to do is to pick oneself up and try to go on again.' Wittgenstein, *Last pool*, 36

For the birds

But these brief evocations of other times and of places to which I hope to return someday are interim views, hastily drawn like the breaths one takes when resting for a moment in a climb, turning away from close-up engagement with the next step of the slope to look back into the distances already traversed, as if a draught of space were as necessary to the body as air. *Listening to the wind,* 71

The shore drew me on by the mesmeric glittering of its waters; the days of walking became a drug, until I felt I was abandoning myself to the pursuit of this glittering for its own sake, that I welcomed every conceivable complexity of interplay between land and sea. *Setting foot,* 21

Three times in my diaries of the time I spent exploring south Connemara some thirty years ago, I find such exclamations as 'I could wander onwards up here for ever.' And so I should and would if I could; but life is finite and art is infinite, and if I am not only to experience Connemara but to share that experience as well as words will let me, I have to impose a boundary. *Gaelic kingdom,* 253

Claddaghduff / *black shore*

66

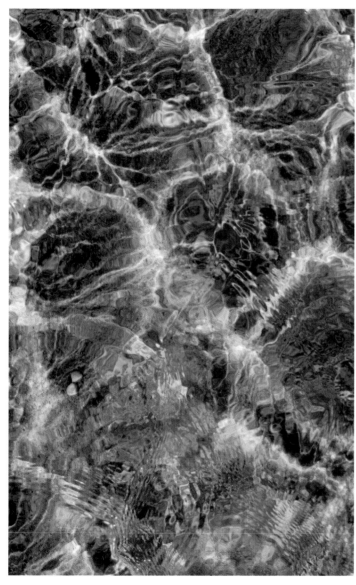

White noise: an outcry inarticulate

In general appearance each map consists of a line and some loops. Any one of them could represent the side of a continent or the margin of a rock pool.

This repetition of form within form, tempting one to credit nature with exuberant prodigality, also occurs in the geometry of river systems, cloud profiles and many other linear features of our world, and is common in matters of area too. Consider a rocky Connemara island; its area might be given on a map as so many acres, but that is to ignore its approximately pyramidal form. One can make an adjustment for this; and then one is on the slope, if not to infinity, then to the indefinitely huge. The slanting sides of the pyramid are of course complicated by cliffs and gullies, and these by jutting rocks and sheep-worn paths, all these surfaces being grooved and pitted and rough with crystals, and so on down to the craggy microcosms an ant has to toil over; all these features immeasurably increase one's estimate of the island's area, and there is no obvious stopping place in this hopeless pursuit of accuracy. The natural world is largely composed of such recalcitrant entities, over which the geometry of Euclid, the fairytale of lines, circles, areas and volumes we are told at school, has no authority.

Some of these apparently anomalous phenomena had been puzzled over by mathematicians before him, but the man who brought them together as objects of empirical study and theorization, and finally unified the field by the brilliant conceptual invention of the fractal, was the mathematician Benoît Mandelbrot; the question with which I opened this preface pays homage to his famous paper of 1967, 'How Long Is the Coast of Britain?' Mandelbrot named his invention with an eye to the Latin, *fractus*, broken. He gives a precise mathematical definition of a fractal, but also allows for a looser use of the term to cover the sort of things considered above, such as coastlines, that exhibit a degree of self-similarity over a range of scales and are therefore too complicated to be described in terms of classical geometry, which would indeed regard them as broken, confused, tangled, unworthy of the dignity of measure. His mathematically perfect fractals inhabit the Platonic world of forms, and relate to naturally occurring fractals as do Euclid's ideal spheres, circles and straight lines to their imperfect counterparts in reality.

One of Mandelbrot's perfect fractals is simple enough to be discussed in prose, I believe, and can be seen as an idealized model of a coastline. It is constructed step by step starting from a straight line, to which what I will call a sidestep is applied; smaller sidesteps are then applied to each straight bit of the first one, then smaller ones still to each straight bit of the result, and so on to the infinitesimally small, so that if one examined any part of it under a magnifying glass or the most powerful of microscopes, it would look the same, sidesteps upon sidesteps for ever:

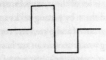

Such an entity is more than a line, which has one dimension, its length, and yet it is not quite an area either, with two dimensions, length and breadth. In fact Mandelbrot showed that it is possible to assign it a dimensionality of one and a half. (I attempt, if not to prove this, then

...to make it sound plausible, in the footnote or optional sidestep below.*)
Gaelic kingdom, 249–251

The reason for the prevalence of fractals in the natural world, very broadly stated, is this: mathematically self-similar structures are the result of applying a procedure to a simple initial entity, then applying the same procedure to the result, and so on – an iterative process, as in the example of sidesteps applied to the results of previous sidesteppings, etc.; and nature itself applies its transforming powers again and again to the outcome of previous transformations, thus bringing into being forms that are self-similar over a wide range of scales and of a degree of complexity that pre-Mandelbrot geometry cannot model. Of course nature's operations are usually multiple, various, random and intermittent, and will throw up exceptions to any generalization. Some of Mandelbrot's constructions involve an element of randomness or statistical variation and achieve much closer likenesses to natural phenomena than does the simple repetitive algorithm of sidesteps mentioned above to a real coastline.

Mandelbrot's collation of two ideas, self-similarity and fractional dimensionality, opened up new vistas of thought. What had been an obscure speculation in pure mathematics suddenly became important in physics, the earth sciences, biology and astrophysics, and has proved crucial to one of the great intellectual breakthroughs of the last century, the founding of our ominous new disciplines, Complexity, Catastrophe and Chaos. It also promises to be a rich source of metaphor and imagery in literature and art. Like all discoveries it surprises us yet again with the unfathomable depth and richness of the natural world; specifically it shows that there is more space, there are more places, within a forest, among the galaxies or on a Connemara seashore, than the geometry of common sense allows. *Gaelic kingdom*, 252

The Inordinate Isles

Scale: one inch to the mile (1 : 63360)

If Plato is right and the things of this world are imperfect copies of ideal forms, then the archipelago of Na hOileáin, the islands, must have its celestial counterpart in a realm of absolute goodness, beauty and truth. In a wild flight of fancy, born of hard days of bog-hopping and shore-stumbling, I came to associate it with the mathematical object known as the Mandelbrot set. This astounding form was first evoked in 1980 by the genius who gave us the concept of the fractal. As it was built up for the first time, pixel by pixel on a primitive computer screen through the endless reiteration of a very simple calculation, it loomed into view, slowly revealing more and more of its details. Its initial bug-like appearance as a kidney-shaped region with a circular bud just touching it at its round end, and vague spindly antennae, was not engaging. But then its finer features gradually became visible, or perhaps, one should say, came into existence. Its boundary proved to be studded with circular buds like the first but ranging downwards in size to invisibility. With today's computers one can see that each of these buds is rimmed by endless numbers of lesser ones, and so on ad infinitum, all of them issuing in filaments that ramify, coil into exquisite curlicues and clasp together like barbaric ornaments. Choose any tiny fragment of this tissue of forms and magnify it a thousand-fold, or a million-fold, and you find inexhaustible treasures: hyperdaisies, superCeltic spirals, spilt galaxies, celestial seaweed beds. Caught in this paradisal tangle like jewelled clasps in the hair of archangels are countless reduced versions of the original set, each of which has its own ever-more-minute simulacra, down to the infinitesimally small, giving the whole a degree of self-similarity that makes it the mother of all fractals. A flight into the endless complexities of this psychedelic fantasia through the medium of the computer screen is one of the signature experiences of this age, an enchantment, revelatory of the richness of pure form, and mortally frightening.

NA hOILEÁIN

And on the other hand, one has the messy confusion of Na hOileáin, the result of repeated geological faulting and the ever-renewed attack of the ocean. One can pick form out of it, including a notable degree of self-similarity in the hierarchical concatenation of its islands. Garomna, a battered disc some four miles across, is its heart. At the north, north-west and south-west, Garomna is linked by causeways to rather smaller islands, each of them linked to two or three still-smaller ones. Every one of these islands has an irregular halo of islets and offshore rocks, many of which can be reached when the tide is out. The fringes of these exhibit the usual interdigitation and mutual inclusion of sea and shore: headlands riven by creeks, bays forking around promontories, rock pools with rocky hummocks standing in them, rocky hummocks with rock pools hollowed out of them. Nevertheless, to compare the general form of the archipelago with that of the Mandelbrot set exposes it as stunted, lopsided, ridiculous, falling far short of the Platonic ideal. But this is to read it as a mere outline on a map, and if the cartographical image is abandoned in favour of direct physical contact with the place, supplemented by attention to its unwearying account of itself in placelore and song, the actual asserts its superior powers of fascination. So I will indulge my extravagant comparison, and erect the Mandelbrot set as a little folly from which to survey this ultimate extravagance of Connemara's topography.

The true fractal, washed in the streams of pure thought, is a hierarchical structure, each level of which contains a lower level – with the paradoxical feature that all the levels are identical; enter, and there is no way of telling what level you are at. In the next chapter I visit, among many other places, a *glasoileán*, a tidal almost-island that is accessible at low water from a certain islet that itself is subsidiary to an island that is, because it is almost deserted, a social appendage of a well-inhabited island that is functionally part of the mainland by virtue of a causeway. Common sense, science and art tell me to discriminate between these levels, to allot each only its due share in my book. If I sometimes neglect this sensible advice it is because of echoes from those other levels, up to the planetary (explicit, as will become clear in my explorations of Na hOileáin) and down to the subatomic (implicit here but salient elsewhere in the book), echoes that inform and perhaps confuse my consciousness of the scales of everyday.

Since the softening cover of peat has long ago been stripped off these islands and burned in the hearths of Aran, Galway and County Clare, one level of reality is immediate and demanding. Treeless, rugged, low-horizoned, the terrain directs attention to what is underfoot. Oddities and anomalies of bedrock and boulders have been exhaustively commented on, named, explained by myths. The bleak outer reaches of the archipelago – the southern third of Garomna, the southern half of Leitir Móir, the ultimate westernmost island, Gólam – are of a geology so visibly different from the pale glistening granite of the rest, so dark, crabbed, written-through with ancient catastrophes, that it demands elucidation (and is in fact evidence of the collision of two continents). All this, with a patchy cloak of humanity thrown over it: roads, villages (dozens of them), old churches, trades (kelp, boats, poitín), ill-remembered history, well-remembered songs…

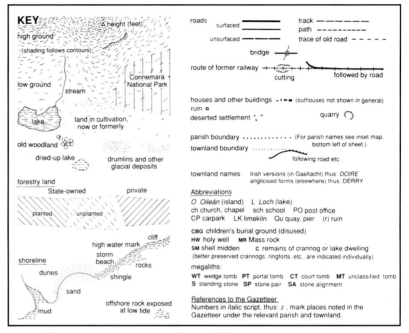

Details from *Connemara map*, this and facing page

To make sense of it all – but no, to make sense of it would be to belittle it; let me say, to avoid total bewilderment and paralysis at its innumerable crossroads – I must follow a simple topographical trend, and thread any temporal diversions, whether into personal reminiscences or geological millennia, onto that one spatial continuity. Like any bicycle-borne visitor I'll enter the maze from the north-east, where it is linked by a causeway to the mainland, and work my way down and around to its south-western extremity. *Gaelic kingdom, 315–317*

But ultimately I accept the complication, the obstacle to writing, with gratitude; it widens the boundary region between established truth and unstable imaginings that is my preferred territory and through which my book prowls to its conclusion. *Listening to the wind*, 375

This handling of the spirit of the rock pool [the rock-fish] made me conscious of the immensity of the hidden interface between land and sea. A fish the size of the *donnánach* has access to holes and crevices the surface area of which is many times greater than that of the foreshore as we would measure it, in acres, say. Within those retreats are smaller ones, home to little creeping things that enjoy still larger areas, not just in inverse proportion to their own size, but absolutely. Extending this thought to the single-celled population of the seashore, it seems that our acre contains within it thousands of acres. Since thought has access everywhere, rightly considered the nondescript rocky shore is cavernous, labyrinthine, unfathomable. Add to these fractal dimensions the echoing linguistic space opened up by placenames and oral lore, and the mythic realms inhabited by prophetic fish and wonder-working saints, and it is clear that my account of it, even if I wrote volumes on this one dog-eared corner of land, would be a mere footnote to reality. *Gaelic kingdom*, 300

Seáinín also showed me a dyke of blackish rock cutting westwards through the blonde granite of the shore, which he said was the way a saint took to Mac Dara's holy island, according to the *seanchas*, the old lore passed down by the *seandream*, the old folk. (Of all the words in the Irish language the most potent are *sean*, old, and *siar*, westwards or backwards in time or space. Some might say they are the two great bugbears of the nation, but I have written this book to celebrate their unquenched energy and mutual intrication.) We talked of the offshore rocks too. Nearby was the Bruiser Rock, which was discovered the hard way by the *Bruiser*, a British gunboat, when distributing food around the famished islands in the 1880s. Further out I could see dozens of others, each of which, I knew, would be the anchor stone for a web of stories set, most of them, in the half-dimension of things not to be believed in but to be wondered at. Tokens of the inexhaustible fractality of both the real and the imaginary, they challenged the art of words. Every tale entails the tale of its own making, generalities breed exceptions as soon as they are stated, and all footnotes call for footnoting, to the end of the world. So, discourse being fractal and life brief, I will let the saint's black shortcut lead me between those rocks and over the waves to his island, from which it is no distance at all to my own home. *Gaelic kingdom*, 380

But the saint's staff or *bachal*, the shepherd's crook, is itself a question-mark. *Setting foot*, 159

Verity's anchor

My connection with all this was that I had written a few pages on the visit Artaud made to the Aran Islands in 1937, when he was already on the cusp of madness. He was in search of the last descendants of the druids, and also wished to return to Ireland a staff that he believed to have belonged to St Patrick.

Last pool, 185

But, trying to understand afterwards how it was that I had come home with little or nothing of interest about her own childhood in Aughrus, I realize that my concept of a walk, which almost precludes talk except of the immediate data of landscape-consciousness, had imposed itself. And it was as if Olwen had literally gone along with this determination of the occasion, leaving me as free within it as if I had been alone (which was in fact my abiding impression of the afternoon). That she was able to do this, without having to think about it or make any effort, demonstrates that she is neither self-effacing nor overbearing; she exactly occupies her own space. Perhaps she had brilliantly performed the role of nobody, as in my first conception of her. Looking back on our circuit of Aughrus and its central lake, I only know that I had felt the presence of a lake of stillness within her.

Last pool, 193

The boneyard in the mist

Letterfrack Industrial School for Boys burial ground

The old world, so far sunk into desuetude that it is hardly distinguishable from the other world of ghosts and fairies, still subsists in nettly banks and briary ditches in the interstices of the modern. I used to enquire…after children's burial grounds, having found that almost every townland or village had one tucked away in some unfrequented or marginal spot, unrecorded and in danger of being itself buried, not in ground consecrated by grief but in concrete of foundations. *Gaelic kingdom,* 313

Often a stillborn child would be buried by night in some ancient earthwork whose origins as a stockyard around a dwelling had been forgotten for centuries and which bore an anomalous otherworldly repute as a fairy fort, or under a fence between two properties, as if neither side would accept responsibility for it, or on the no man's land of the seashore. *Listening to the wind,* 93–94

CBG (see key page 71)

The depth of field

I like fossicking and yoricking about in graveyards, scanning the headstones, stopping for a closer look at one or another, as one takes down a book from a bookshop shelf to see if its opening words live up to its title. One of my desiderata for a well-run world would be that every tombstone carry a brief biography (and, at the foot, 'For notes and sources, see over'). *Listening to the wind, 98*

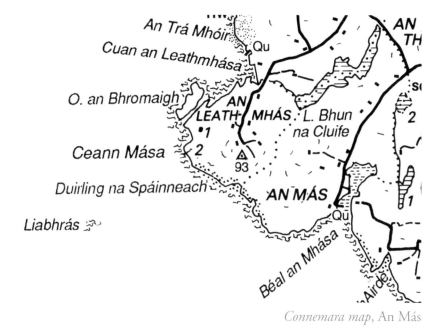

Connemara map, An Más

Emigration, though, is the face in the windows of empty houses throughout Connemara. *Setting foot, 71*

Dresser

78

Here Farrell lived, a tailor; here he sat with his scissors, thimble and, instead of a tape measure, a bit of sheepskin, according to what I have been told of the work methods of Connemara tailors, who used to record the measurements of each client by holding up a straight edge of a sheepskin against him or her and marking off the lengths on it with little snips. When the garments were finished a strip would be cut off the sheepskin to leave a fresh edge for the next job. Similarly Time, the tailor of all things, snipped strips off Farrell's lifespan until nothing was left, and then off that of his house, and then off all remembrance of him or his house, of which I hereby salvage this one narrow strip. *Listening to the wind*, 21

Dislocation

Without the occasional renewal of memory and regular rehearsal of meaning, place itself founders into shapelessness, and time, the great amnesiac, forgets all. *Gaelic kingdom*, 69

Connemara map, detail

History has rhythms, tunes and even harmonies; but the sound of the past is an agonistic multiplicity. *Listening to the wind*, 2

I have a snapshot I took (curious art, that conserves me a memory of an occasion in which I seemingly do not figure – thus showing how things will be when I am gone). *Gaelic kingdom*, 297

Then I sounded them for Broughton history. At first all I got was what they had read up the night before in one of my own publications, an echo-effect that haunts me in Connemara these days. *Listening to the wind*, 138

An Chnapach, though, is long deserted; the McDonaghs sold it to a local man who has built a large concrete causeway out to it, erected an ugly cattle shed and put up notices: 'Keep out' and 'Beware of the bull'. I found the ruins of the old shop, with a little quay below it. The island is largely rocky hummocks and marshy hollows, and when I was down in one of the latter I heard two men talking; I was surprised, as I thought I had the place to myself. But when I ran up the knoll and looked around, nobody was there. I recounted this event as a ghost story in the house I was staying in at the time; it caused quite a sensation, and I hope it has become part of the lore of the lumpy island. Adapted from *Gaelic kingdom*, 372–373

Bullish diptych, Cathair an Dúin / the fort of the bluff

Galvanized

All the mountain-land extent of Gabhla and the townlands south of it used to be open countryside, but now it is patched with forestry and there are some annoying fences across it, too high to step over. How do I treat these? If no stile is provided, the barbed wire implicitly says, 'No trespassers'. But if there were no such prohibitions there would be no such thing as trespassing. So I can do the landowner a favour by ignoring his fences. And thus, by logical wizardry, I find myself on the other side of the fence. *Gaelic kingdom*, 238

The horizon, then, is where the possible and the impossible meet. Did it also impress me as an all-encircling threat? *My time in space*, 12

But nearly all the interesting and beautiful items of my close-up view of Connemara lie on private land or on commonage, access to which is controlled by the group of farmers who use it and who can decide to fence it off.... However, there was in general no difficulty about crossing farmland until the enormous increase, over the last decade or so, in the numbers of ramblers, some of them ignorant or careless of the practicalities of working the land. Now we need dialogue, mutual understanding, sensible legislation, etc. – rare panaceas – and, much deeper, a shared sense of the Earth's surface as a palimpsest, the compiled and over-written testaments of all previous generations, which it is our right and duty to read. When I come to enquire into the monuments and marks that have been set on this little facet of it,...I realize how much of the history of Connemara is covered by the question of who owns the land. It is a story of interventions...rather than a story generated by Connemara itself. Those interventions are the generalities that impose a periodization on the story – but humanity is in the details, and to read it properly we need to attend to the small print of that vast document. *Last pool*, 290–291

Now the relics of past times, which are principally those of past owners, their powers, pieties and sorrows, are reduced to cattle-pens on the farmer's land. Property rights and possessive attitudes cut us off from even these disparaged stones, leaving us as flimsy as paper figures cut out of our backgrounds in history and nature. Where do we turn, to find a way of looking at the land, inhabiting it, loving it, other than that of ownership? *Last pool*, 307

Walking the horizon

Hear the difference between 'Captain O'Malley' and, properly pronounced, 'An Caiptín Máilleach' – it is as if the syllables of Irish have more space inside them. In fact there are Irish words so spacious you could hold a *céilí* dance in one syllable and a wake in another, without mutual interference. The art that explores these spaces inside words is *sean-nós*. In print, and in translation, I can only explore the outsides of such words. *Last pool*, 109

Puzzled S

To the north of the road, the uninspiring tarmac deserts and one-storey boxes of an Údarás na Gaeltachta industrial estate. *Gaelic kingdom*, 204

Northside Carna

85

Féichín's well

From St Féichín's invocation of the plague to Richard Murphy's love affair with loneliness, the dangerous equations argued by High Island are those between humanity and pollution, society and contamination, companionship and distraction from the eternal. Even if we feel that the eternal can well look after itself – for it has time on its hands – we might be made uneasy by that sterile orb, glinting in the harsh light of High Island's associations. Is it a prevision of the Earth's future? In St Féichín's time, that pool of medieval darkness, things may have seemed clearer, but nowadays we cannot distinguish plague from people, there being so many too many of us. *Last pool,* 208

Watching High

Washed-up

H and per se and S

Collectable as some items of it may be, the cumulative effect of this Gulf Stream of garbage is deeply disturbing; it reads as the signature of a worldwide calamity, a breakdown of due process, a resentment of the ocean's superhuman purity. *Listening to the wind*, 247

Nowadays, with so much of its surface in wreckage and filth, it is the Earth that faces us with moral demands. The spiritual merges once again with the natural, from which, disastrously, it has been separated for some centuries. *My time in space*, 203

As we well know, some future environmental Armageddon could lead to a world without mind. And that vanishing is a possibility we are not entirely reluctant to entertain, because of our guilt in the face of Nature. *My time in space*, 182–183

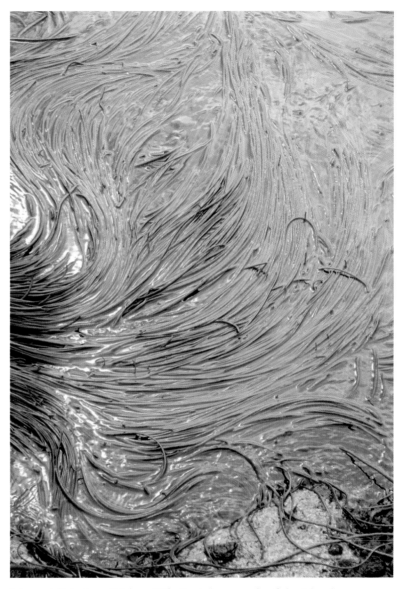

Mermaid's hair at Béal an Oileáin / the mouth of the island

By then humanity, if it could still be so called, will be existing without Nature, almost without reality. Our consciousnesses will have been amalgamated, compressed and downloaded onto the galactic internet. Every atomic particle will ultimately be pressed into service for our databank, until there is nothing in the universe but information. *My time in space,* 183

Nevertheless, and to extract myself from the bogs of philosophy, it is a curious realization that we are all now suffused by messages, in a way that did not obtain in the past. Marconi in Derrigimlagh represents a crucial step in the filling of the bath of invisible communications we are all immersed in today, the electromagnetic fever and silent cacophony of words and images passing through us at every moment. The most common message, the one we are most urgent to impart, is and has been since the days of the megalith-builders, 'I'm here...', wherever that may be; 'I am here, now – therefore I exist. And you know it, so I belong to the human race.' *Last pool,* 274–275

The Irish Times, Saturday, July 30th, 2005, at Féar Milis / sweet grass, Friday, June 1st, 2012, 19:38'46"

In the west of Ireland are territories where a proportion is still preserved; nature has room for its ways and so does humanity. This sphere of interaction and qualified autonomies has its echoes and the echo hunters necessary to their awakening, its sheerest cliffs have names and histories, its placelore knows a gradation of familiarity from town centre to lonely upland. Without defining it more tightly, I'll call it the Echosphere; the word has been lying around in my mind for years awaiting an application.

Descending to the local and personal scale of my time in the west of Ireland, which has coincided with a surge of economic growth, I am as aware of cultural loss, loss of history, loss of echo, as I am of ecological damage. I have come to resent the truth-telling of environmentalism; a sense of the Earth's vulnerability and of the obligation to defend it hangs a veil of anxiety between me and the landscape. At every turn of my walks I expect to find some detail of the scene that I have lovingly and scrupulously noted in one of my maps or books, effaced by careless 'improvement': a JCB levelling a site for a house has needlessly scooped away an old limekiln; a road-widening scheme has heaped rubble onto a stone commemorating the death of a friar at the hands of priest-hunters. Is it mere ignorance and indifference, or does some wordless animosity drive this destruction of the countryside and the little landmarks that make it meaningful? *My time in space*, 176

By the time we returned to St Cáillín's Island the girls were swimming off a cobbly beach of its western shore, observed by half a dozen seals – goggle-eyed old gentlemen voyeurs – whose heads showed above the waves at a little distance. The twin sister-and-brother blues of sky and ocean, the gold and black of the rocks, the vaporous apparition of the lighthouse island out to the west with its mysterious towers, one of them bearing the intermittent spark that marks the ultimate reach of Connemara, all astounded me yet again. The swimmers had the right of it, I briefly felt: total unreflecting immersion in the flux of the world, as opposed to my grain-by-grain hoarding of detail. If I was right, then this book might as well be thrown into the sea. But as we began to assemble below the chapel again and the dinghy came and went, the lovely generalities were enhanced and enchanted, and my ways vindicated, by the strangest of details: the iridescent, slightly undulant layer of the by-the-wind sailors lay on the waters like a throng of pilgrims with faces upturned to a cathedral balcony: or perhaps they were the souls – no, better, the last breaths, caught in silver and blue bubbles – of all the fisherfolk who had ever been drowned in these waters, gathered here to confront the saint who could not save them. Another ravishing detail: long thin fronds of orange-red thong-weed lay among the by-the-wind sailors in coils and Celtic interlacings, making of the water surface an illuminated vellum, a page from that lost *Book of Cáillín*. Adapted from *Last pool*, 335–336

Sensitive surface

Trá Mhíl / whale beach

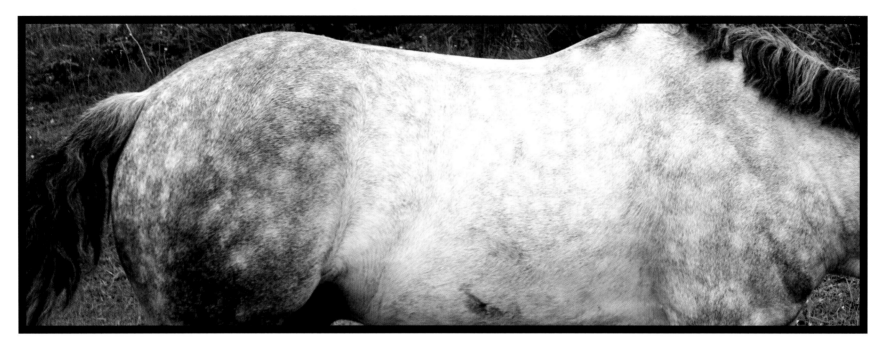

The patches / *na Paistí*

That the simple triangle (or, better, the triangular emptiness) has such weight in this elemental landscape serves to remind me that one can tire of Mandelbrot's fractal epiphanies with their eternal spirals winding into eternity. Perhaps one could claim that fractal geometry is to Celtic art as Euclid is to classical art. While the mainstream of European culture has pursued its magnificent course, another perception has been kept in mind by the Celtic periphery…– in a word, that a fascinating sort of beauty arises out of the repetitive interweaving of simple elements. The beauty of nature is often of this sort. In Connemara, which is pre-eminently the land of 'dappled things' – drizzly skies, bubbly streams, tussocky hills – one recognizes the texture. But after a thorough soaking in this dappled Celtic bewilderment, one is tempted to run for shelter in classical temples. Perhaps this is why I have taken so inordinate an interest in the round and triangular holy wells, treating them as major reference points in a landscape that otherwise teems with ungraspable reiterations of details. Perhaps too something of this same feeling arose in the *seandream*, the old folk of vaguely ancient days, who found and named and speculated about these exceptions to the phenomenological flux, thus adding to the realms of the real and the ideal the imaginary in all its incalculable dimensionality. *Gaelic kingdom, 352–353*

Here lies the image of a well I came across but cannot find anymore, at the bottom of which sat a perfectly shaped round stone that formed a perfect 360° U, taken on that marvellous day when I went wandering with no camera.

nicolas fève

What exactly wells up for me at this moment of writing, in these triangular sources? I used to think it was 'meaning' – but that is a mere gesture, a waving to the reader to come to my help, for meaning is always specific; one can always ask, 'What meaning?' Now I take it to be the primitive precursor of meaning, difference. Without differences, distinctions, discriminations, no world, no language, no meaning. *Gaelic kingdom, 358*

And if the web of associations I have spun around these quaint landmarks in Garomna should lap out beyond the vague confines of Connemara to envelop more and more of the world, it might bring with it the suggestion of a way of looking at places as sources of difference; and surely taking note of the particularities of a place is the first step in taking care of it. *Gaelic kingdom, 359*

I was distracted from my exploration by a water-skater, whose shadow on the bottom of the pond was shaped like a four-leafed clover. It seemed at least marginally comprehensible that this minute display of clockwork jewellery should be staged by sunlight and insect and the laws of refraction to the delight of my eye, since I happened to be passing by, but not that it should be happening unobserved in a million sun-drenched pools all over the bogs at that moment; to be an ambulant point of view is a familiar mystery, but the existence of infinities of untenanted potential points of view is a destabilizing thought. Adapted from *Listening to the wind*, 67–68

At home I did occasionally notice a visitor's gaze, idly straying across blank surfaces, suddenly arrested as a reflex of sight focused attention on one of the dots I had set like traps around our rooms; then I would know that a moment had been picked up, salvaged from the blind onrush of time, that an unknown significance had arisen, like the curl of a questionmark from a full stop, out of an event almost as bare and minimal as one of relativity theory's space-time data. *My time in space*, 69

Like any other animal, each of us is the embodied origin of a particular perspective on time and space. 'Land without shortcuts', 38

Still surface

Still pane

What is it that comes into existence as you step into it and ceases to exist when you step out? The exact answer is your life, of course; but an island is an approximate answer, only slightly blurred by the aura of expectation extending before one's visit and of memory prolonging it. A little jaded from dipping into so many life-sites, we lay on the quay in the sunshine, and Seán sent Simon off to ask Catherine to come and collect us. I was unsure as to whether I should offer Pádraic money or not, and asked Seán to sound him out. Pádraic politely declined payment, saying, '*Ní dhéanfadh sé saibhir nó daibhir mé*' – 'It wouldn't make me rich or poor.' I was charmed by the grace of this refusal, and by its recourse to the ancient magic of the *so/do* (good/bad) prefixes in the Irish language. *Solas/dolas*, bright/dark; *soiléir/doiléir*, distinct/obscure; *soineann/doineann*, fair weather/stormy weather; *sólás/dólás*, solace/dolour…I could map all my island findings and feelings in such twinned opposites. *Gaelic kingdom, 203*

That the basis of existence is difference, that the first step in understanding is discrimination, is for me an axiom that feels as if it were innate. *My time in space, 147*

In fact it was the experience of 'walking out to islands', specifically Fínis and Inis Bearcháin, in Na hOileáin, that first shocked me into, if not poetry, then poetic prose on the subject of Connemara, in 1981….Coming to write about Fínis once again, I realize that writing about an experience is a way of forgetting it, or perhaps of sacrificing it for the sake of writing, for the memory of what one has written overwrites one's memory of the event that inspired the writing. In any case, since I cannot recapture my anything-but-careless if rapturous prose style of earlier years, I will now have to find my way into the island in a more objective mood.

Shifting sands and the timetable of tides necessarily dominate all thought of Fínis. *Gaelic kingdom, 194*

With an island, it is as if the surrounding ocean like a magnifying glass directs an intensified vision onto the narrow field of view. A little piece is cut out of the world, marked off in fact by its richness in significances. So an island appears to be mappable. Already a little abstracted from reality, already half-concept, it holds out the delusion of a comprehensible totality. *Setting foot, 1*

Omey Strand

Walking on Sunday into Omey Island
When the tide had fallen slack.
I crossed a spit of wet ribbed sand
With a cold breeze at my back.

Richard Murphy

Space…is, among everything else, the interlocking of all our mental and physical trajectories, good or ill, through all the subspaces of experience up to the cosmic. *Setting foot*, vi

And since for centuries the material world was seen as a quarry of metaphors to describe the glories of a spiritual world, that gorgeous structure of the imagination should in return provide the liturgy and ceremonial we need for a praiseful approach to the places that glorify the here below. 'Land without shortcuts', 43–44

The long languorous hip-and-waist-like curve of the skyline of Cnoc Mordáin to the east, which he called the Sleeping Beauty.

Listening to the wind, 237

What is the role, nowadays, of this rumpled bed of a metaphor? Most trivially, it is a slightly disguised, displaced or sublimated sexual fantasy…More important is its gender-asymmetry….A metaphor is a bridge intended to carry meaning across from one topic to another – but as soon as the bridge is established, meaning will sneak across it in the other direction, unobserved….

It may be that the imagery I have been discussing derives its power, pathos and persuasiveness from an illicit appeal to a supernaturalist mode of thought I reject. Liberating the saints and their miraculous wells from their rags of historicity, I use them as poetic expressions of the powers of nature – but does their relict sanctity infect my poetry with untruth? Is the idea of a sacred landscape still viable?…The Burren claims attention in its own right through its many singularities, not as a pointer to something transcending it…. And if the Earth appears to revenge itself for our violations, as it may be doing already through global warming, it is as a self-adjusting system of feedback loops, not as a conscious being acting with intent….

So, what I would like to find is a language for these questions, not dependent on personalizing the land, neither sexualizing nor spiritualizing my relationship with it. To date, all I have towards that is what I have written about in *Stones of Aran* and elsewhere, the act of walking. To me, walking is a way of expressing, acting out, a relationship to the physical world; there are of course many others, notably in art. This sort of walking is an intense cognitive and physical involvement with the terrain, close to but not lapsing into identification with it, not a mysticism; and not a matter of getting from A to B but of lingering, revisiting, cross-hatching an area with one's most alert and best–informed attention. And my maps are the lasting traces of such mobiles reveries; they are drawn in footprints. Sometimes, looking back on the times they represent for me, I feel they have been dreamed in footprints. *My time in space*, 101, 102, 103

Sleeping beauty

Origin of species

102

Our wastelands are so beautiful and so tender we wonder if we should enter them at all. Should we stand here discussing the origins of the bog, knowing that a footprint in sphagnum moss lasts a year or more, that the tuft of lichen we crush unseeingly has taken decades to grow? Sometimes when a snipe leaps from under my feet and goes panicking up the sky, I am appalled at my own presence in a place so old and slow and long-suffering as Roundstone Bog. *Listening to the wind*, 56–57

Apart from its ecological uniqueness, Roundstone Bog harbours one of the rarest of resources, solitude. Adapted from *My time in space*, 195

A bog is its own diary; its mode of being is preservation of its past. The current page is the brightest and fullest, but whatever grows and dies on the surface, together with whatever is blown into it from neighbouring areas, will be pickled in the acidic waters, buried under the remains of future years' growth and added to the layered record. *Listening to the wind*, 47

ridge of rock and heather, which turns out to be a promontory ending in more sedge swamp. All this can produce weariness and anxiety, but it is pure delight when the weather is good, the evenings are long and there is no need to hurry. Sometimes I come back from such a walk with my head so empty it seems not a single thought or observation has passed through it all day, and I feel I have truly seen things as they are when I'm not there to see them. *Listening to the wind*, 25–26

Looking into the distance on heading into the bog, one's first impressions are of monotony and uniformity, but experience soon undoes that, through the constant recalling of attention to what is underfoot or immediately ahead by the difficulties of progress. The most serious obstacles are the flat areas where water glints between clumps of sedge; one is tempted to hop from tussock to tussock, but is forced to backtrack when they become too far apart; then one detours onto a hummocky area pitted with bog-holes and, after struggling with that for a while, scrambles onto a promising-looking

I could, I suppose, turn to my reference books and scientific offprints and write sensibly about Roundstone Bog, outlining its topography and hydrography, its archaeology and ecology, history of land-use and current problems of conservation. But I prefer to imagine walks across it, enmeshing the reader in its textures, letting the generalities emerge when the pressure of detail compels them. Adapted from *Listening to the wind*, 21

'I know all this is hundreds of thousands of years old,' said Connor, stamping on the bare peat of the new bench, as eager to learn from me as I from him, 'and they say it was all forest here long ago; but what is this stuff? Compressed trees?' I explained that the bogs started to grow perhaps three thousand years ago and were only intermittently forested, and that the peat is the remains of much the same sorts of plants that grow on the bog today. That prompted a curious thought: if the bottom of, say, a six-spit-deep bog is three thousand years old, then one end of a sod of turf is five hundred years older than the other. Suddenly the sods appeared to me as compass needles torn out of their natural alignment in the time-field, their orientation to the centre of the earth. *Listening to the wind*, 60–61

My favoured mode of walking being not a single-minded goal-bound linear advance but a cross-questioning of an area, or even a deliberate seeking out of the *fóidín mearaí*, the 'stray sod' that is said to put anyone who treads on it wandering. *Listening to the wind*, 364

We are all prone to error, we are all strangers on our own land. *Setting foot*, 159

The depth of the surface

Plane surface

The fractals that pass…over there…over there…

For I do not know that I understand what I have written. No; I am writing blind, as a pilot has to fly blind in fog or cloud, sustained by faith in a compass course rather than by vision of a destination. But this much is clear: the recommended situation for cultivation of the compass rose is on the very edge of the cliff. *Setting foot*, 107

I know that the step, which is only one in a linked set of images of lateral extension – the walk, the path, the labyrinth, the spider's web – is not some poetic flower picked of my own creative fancy by the wayside of my life, because, looking back, I see it implicit in the art works I made in London before I came to Ireland. Adapted from *Setting foot*, 213

The print of nature

Old ladies of Carna who worked in the Lace School when they were young remembered picking the flower-heads of bog-cotton to make the fillings for lace-covered buttons. Adapted from *Mapping South Connemara*, 23

What I am trying to recapture is how the people of Connemara felt their countryside, how they read it. It was like a book in fineness of detail, closeness of print; every corner of it conveyed a message, held a memory. *Setting foot*, 166

As I said, the most revealing features of a map are its blank areas. I think that is one reason I prefer to build up my maps of little dots and strokes of the pen standing separately on blank paper, rather than layers of colour that cover whole areas and implicitly claim to say something about every point within them. In the nature of fractals, the closest and most detailed exploration or mapping imaginable cannot do more than scratch the surface. My mode of drawing is a scratching of the surface of the paper, and makes no claims to comprehensiveness. Because of the psychological carry-over mentioned earlier, from my repetitive footsteps to this repetitive handwork, it is also a caressing of the Earth, a soothing and taming of the fractious fractal itself.

Discourse, too, is fractal; every remark suggests amplifications and amendments, every thesis, critiques and refutations; this fractal nature of intertextuality is the clue to the way the text itself sits into the fractals of non-textual reality. *Setting foot*, 102

At home: *The last pool of darkness*, 215; *'Hexagon'*; Hexagon

enclosure with a wall nearly two yards high, partly already lost to the sea, with a mass burial of about forty-five bodies within it. Two *leachta*, low stone altars, with white quartz pebbles on them, were found too, one on top of the other, and two cross-inscribed slabs have subsequently been found among the masonry tumbled on the foreshore below the sand cliff. Three hundred yards to the east, to complete this brief necrology of necropolises, there is another long-disused burial ground by the shoreline called Cnocán na mBan, the hillock of the women, which was reserved for women only. The saint's mother is said to lie in it – but bones are surfacing here and melting away under the rain in the course of the sand's restless workings, so perhaps the good lady has already contributed her mite to the endless recycling of material between land and sea.

Having poked reverently around these boneyards we moved on eastwards and looked at the former national schoolhouse, opened in 1883, closed in 1973 because of the dwindling number of scholars and now made into a holiday home. Near it is the odd little flat-roofed one-room house Richard Murphy built in 1974, sitting like a hexagonal nut bolt upright on a little height, as a scriptorium for times when it was too rough for him to sail out to High Island, Omey offering a compromise between hermetic inaccessibility and car-borne convenience:

The bed filled one of the six walls opposite a golden-rectangular window facing north with a view across a shallow sound to Aughrus-more. A sink and a gas cooker filled the wall under a window looking down across the strand, where, on a rising tide, I could watch the two arms of the sea join to embrace the island for five hours and part to release it from isolation on the ebb . . . Whenever I entered, harassed by rain, wind and the anxieties of life on the mainland, the figure of the hexagon, repeated like a musical theme with variations in the walls, the table and the ceiling, calmed me with a sense of concentricity and gave me the centripetal energy I needed to sit down, take out a notebook, and write.

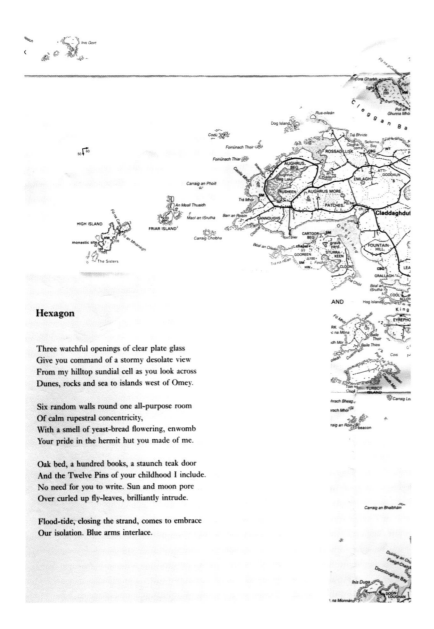

Hexagon

Three watchful openings of clear plate glass
Give you command of a stormy desolate view
From my hilltop sundial cell as you look across
Dunes, rocks and sea to islands west of Omey.

Six random walls round one all-purpose room
Of calm rupestral concentricity,
With a smell of yeast-bread flowering, enwomb
Your pride in the hermit hut you made of me.

Oak bed, a hundred books, a staunch teak door
And the Twelve Pins of your childhood I include.
No need for you to write. Sun and moon pore
Over curled up fly-leaves, brilliantly intrude.

Flood-tide, closing the strand, comes to embrace
Our isolation. Blue arms interlace.

A secular version of holy wells might call forth an awareness of the place's constitution, the causal net that brought it into existence, from cosmic origins to the casual touch of local microhistory. On such occasions the basic act of attention that creates a place out of a location would be renewed, enhanced by whatever systems of understanding we can muster, from the mathematical to the mythological, by the passion of poetry, or by simple enjoyment of the play of light on it. Here is a gateway to a land without shortcuts, where each place is bathed in the sunlight of our contemplation and all its particularities brought forth, like those mountainside potato plots gilded by midwinter sunset in the valley of the stone alignment. Adapted from 'Land without shortcuts', 43

Lettergesh East-West

The [standing] stone [of Garraunbawn] itself is as it always was and as a physical object needs no restoration; the restoration of its meaning as a contemporary monument, an icon of the locality's specificity, is the task of the topographer and a touch in the restoration of our eroded modern consciousness of place. But what of its original significance in the life-world of those who set it up? *Last pool,* 127 So, at that moment, looking through the hedge at the old stone horse cropping the grass on the hilltop, I could tie together a geological and an archaeological strand of Connemara's prehistory, and follow the efforts of later generations to make sense of that mysterious stone, first by means of a legend of an otherworldly horse, and then by tidying up that story already half forgotten and fossilized in a placename, which itself was later to be misunderstood and gelded by officialdom. *Last pool,* 127 In the absence of radiocarbon dates or of

An Gearrán Bán / the white gelding

funds for proper archeological digs, mental reconstruction and stylistic case the present position of every terms of the original form of the *Last pool,* 133 Those who brought much about death; they perhaps the house of death should be from cycle of life and death interlinks moon. *Last pool,* 134 The quartz and call attention to themselves territorial as birdsong: 'We are this lowland it oversees are ours.' of midsummer half-light the whisper to the imagination, 'You Ghosts and fairies are moods and Earth; they wax and wane with our of white quartz, dim afterlife of its all depended on visual inspection, categorization of the tombs; in each stone had to be accounted for in tomb and its mode of collapse. these great stones together thought debated as to whether entrance to the east or the west, that is, how the with those of the sun, stars and stones, which seem to radiate light from afar, may have been as triumphantly here; this hilltop and And sometimes in the hush glimmering stones of Ballynakill cannot see us, but we are still here.' modes of one's feeling for the desires and delusions. The glimmer daytime brilliance, may persist

throughout a long summer evening, but will succumb to the black rainy nights after Hallowe'en. *Last pool,* 135 The dark hollowness of the tomb under the roadside gorsebush says, 'There is nobody here, and you shall be nowhere too.' *Last pool,* 134 Making this mental correction to the spectacle of the midwinter sunset feels like adjusting the focus of an optical instrument, which is what the alignment, taken together with the cleft in the skyline, really is. From this perfectly placed place on the top of the moraine, a panorama of the mountain walls and the wide wild glen offers itself, and on the shortest day of midwinter another perspective opens up like the aperture in the dome of an observatory; one can see halfway to infinity and eternity, not only the dazzling millions of miles to the sun but the three or four thousand years back to the Bronze Age, and the forty-one-thousand-year wobble of the earth's tilted axis. The place is a foothold on a globe that is tumbling through space and time. The prehistoric links us back to the cosmic. Antiquity is the term I'll take to embrace both. 'Land without shortcuts', 37–38

Bog-cottons, Lough Inagh Valley

The last of the sunbeams were so intense that, looking along the alignment into the dazzlement, it was hard to make out what was happening.
'Land without shortcuts', 36

We, too, are seeing through prehistoric eyes. For the eye, alert to spatial balances, visual discontinuities, the rhetoric of visibility, of seeing and being seen, vastly predates all cultural constructions on that organic basis. (In the eye, I include as much of the image-processing, pattern-recognizing, neural networks of the visual cortex as is necessary to make good my argument.) The eye is evolution's answer to a potential visual field that is a Darwinian arena of life-opportunities and death-threats. Centrality and marginality, openness and closure, balance and imbalance – these states were branded into our nervous systems as fraught with potentialities long before they were conceptualized. The words I use to convey a sense of this place as elevated above and central within the arena of the valley, respectful but not self-abasing before the cirque of mountains, are modern metaphors for ancient phenomenologies. So: this site marks the intersection of an astronomical constant with a constant of human spatial awareness; it is in itself ceremonious, observant of the geometry of humanity and the heavens. *Setting foot,* 203

But whatever their religious and practical dimensions, the placing of these boulders was an aesthetic act, a response to the sense of place and balance I have credited the prehistoric eye with. The choice of this spot pulls all the forces of the valley together and knots them into a form one can grasp. I'm not talking ley-lines or anything mystical here; nothing more mysterious than art, which is mystery enough for me. A site has been created, around which the terrain assembles itself into a landscape – that is, an area apprehended by the eye, taken from a vantage-point. The

concept of landscape, we know, is of modern origin, and its connections with Enlightment objectivity, with the portraiture of estates and the perspectivism of power-relations, have been much discussed; but the roots of its possibility are in the nature of the eye, an organ trained by stick and carrot to command a sphere of vision. Calendrical functions and religious conceptions wither away with time, but a well-founded aesthetic intervention can grow in stature indefinitely. *Setting foot,* 204

In this talk, the ceremonies of raven and falcon, the setting sun and the shadow of the mountain, the salmon seeking out its origins, the glacier disgorging its burden of rock, the changing obliquity of the ecliptic, have been both metaphors for and instances of the processes of nature, the genderless mutual engendering of time and space. And in presenting them in terms of retinal images, of optical geometry, I have been insinuating the idea that the eye itself has its religion, its sense of relationship to the whole, anterior to, underlying, and outlasting all other cults. I fear that these six boulders in Gleninagh, like six precarious stepping stones, are leading me too far out into the Ineffability of the Absolute, but instead of underpinning all I have said with a reference to innate, pre-cultural, Chomskyesque universal spatial grammars, I will suggest that spacetime is the irreducibly general religious object we share with the Bronze Age and with all future inheritors of the prehistoric eye. And with that, before I fall and drown, I will be silent. *Setting foot,* 208

Stranded hedgehog

Horse point / Aughrus beg

115

In the end I marked the place with a dot and in tiny print the words 'a strange field'. Occasionally I hear from someone who has noticed this cartographic curiosity and gone in search of its objective correlative. Usually they have been unsure whether or not they found what I had found, or what it was they were supposed to see in it – but then there is nothing to be seen in it, just grey emptiness, nodding thistles, an occasional attendance of puzzled visitors on a mystique. I take from this instance another modality of places: strangeness. 'Land without shortcuts', 34

H, sweet grass at Féar Milis

The most immediate connection between language and reality, the one first made by children and by language learners, is that of naming things. Placenames are the interlock of landscape and language. *Setting foot*, 155

This is because placenames are semantically two-pronged; they not only have a referent, like any proper name, i.e. the place they denote, but most of them also have a connotation; they make a condensed or elliptic remark about the place, a description, a claim of ownership, a historical anecdote, even a joke or a curse on it. And so they may only reveal their meaning in the physical and historical context of the place. *Setting foot*, 156

Placenames, whether they exist in the mind of the Irish *seanchaí*, the custodian of traditional lore, or in the memory banks of a database, are only the anchor points of a discourse of place. 'Land without shortcuts', 44

Barbarus hic ego sum

118

qui non intellegor ulli

'Here it is I that am a barbarian, understood by nobody', Ovid, *Tristia*, V, x, 37

119

Imagine a world in which time and space are hardly separated, when there are pools of time landlocked in space and islands of space cut off in time, and everywhere and everywhen is blanketed in a boggy mixture of the two. A hunter-gatherer comes splashing and slipping, sweating and swearing, through this world which is her world, and stops on a little promontory between a sea full of islands and a land full of lakes, to draw breath. And the breath she draws is loathsome, fetid, corrupted. Wedged between sea-licked boulders nearby is a huge carcass. The pioneer picks her way around it delicately, respectfully, never having seen such a monster before, dead or alive; half her tribe could huddle under the vaulted roof of its skeleton. Perhaps her conception of the edge of the future is different from ours: rather than a wave for ever breaking over us from ahead, as it seems to be for us, it may form a mist-circle around her that accompanies her in any direction she chooses. But she might already have an inkling of a beginning here, a tendency for time to trickle in one direction only. She will report to the others what she sees and smells on the promontory of the beast, or of the whale, and the phrase will be repeated, and become a placename, a marker of a place fixed in its place and resistant to the flux of time so that it will be translated from language to passing language, to reach our age as Ros a' Mhíl, the promontory of the whale. *Gaelic kingdom, 269*

A stranded sperm whale on Trá Chóil, Omey Island, photographed at low tide, just after dawn.

These mythological names speak to me of the wonders of this world; the acts of the saints are inward and invisible signs pointing us to outward and visible graces; their interventions in topography – passes opened through hills, rocks sailed from one geology to another, springs summoned forth, pothole fonts hollowed out of granite – stand for the extra dimensions human histories have grafted onto places, particularizing and discriminating them, bringing a supplement of spaciousness to space, a treasure that is lost if memory is allowed to die and place reverts to the relative flatness of its three dimensions. Adapted from *Last pool*, 251

Heimatgefühl, the sense of a homeland, is the term Giselher uses for the feeling induced in us by semi-natural landscapes that are at once open to the hugeness of the sky and rich in their detailed accommodation to human purposes....these landscapes are the epitome of what I have called the Echosphere, the zone in which a balance is maintained between culture and the wild, so that, through daily frequentation and the communal memory of placelore, nature answers to the human voice. *Last pool*, 145–146

Geophany, then, the showing forth of the Earth through all the geophanic arts and sciences, should be our means towards a reformation of values. 'Land without shortcuts', 44

That is one function of my work, this translation of the dense web of place-lore out of speech and memory into the world of books and maps, and it is a troubling aspect of the enterprise. *Setting foot*, 96

At the time I wondered why I had struggled against wind and rain to this last desolate desultory promontory to talk to this man about the most marginal of economic activities; a quarter of a century later I can only hope that the completion of this book will answer that question. *Last pool*, 68

122

Nowhere now here

Often when visitors ask me what they should see in this region I am at a loss. A curious hole in the ground? The memory of an old song about a drowning? Ultimately I have to tell them that this is a land without shortcuts.

Gaelic kingdom, 370

A land without shortcuts

Elsewhere

TIM ROBINSON

Elsewhere

Now that a thirty-year project of interpreting the Aran Islands, the Burren and Connemara through mapping and topographical writing is virtually complete, life in our Connemara home is already taking on the qualities of a memory. Recently when I was giving a talk in a local festival I accidentally said that the second half of my life had been spent writing about Connemara, and a kind friend in the audience voiced the hope that this did not imply that my life was nearing its end. I hastened to assure her that I have always expected a life of three halves. Is this asking too much? Already my mind is turning elsewhere, stylistically as well as geographically. Here are three brief forays into this new terrain. Each relies on an atom of autobiography to spark it off, and thereafter explores a possibility of formal invention.

TR, Roundstone, 2014

Where are the Nows of Yesteryear?

Now that so much time has passed since my childhood I must admit the possibility that the clear image I retain of my grandmother's musical box has long been polished into luminosity by nostalgia. The quaint old device stood on a low occasional table in her little antique shop, overshadowed by towering wardrobes and crowding tallboys but glinting as if with an internal energy. Its simple, almost naive, mechanism fascinated me: a spring-powered contraption like the works of an old clock drove the rotation of a brass cylinder, on which were hundreds of prickles that twanged the teeth of a graduated steel comb, producing hesitant and plaintive melodies. This tender machinery was mounted on a polished wooden base and covered by a lid with glass sides, through which I could admire the tense coiled spring and dark laborious cogs, watch the hypnotically slow turning of the gleaming cylinder, and sense the tiny flexure and straining of a tooth of the dull grey comb as each note was prepared, seemed momentarily to resist being detached from silence, and then yielded with a slight reluctance, like a ripe blackberry plucked from a briar. Years later when I read H.G. Wells' description of the Time Machine, a glittering contraption of bronze and crystal, I was carried back to the fusty old shop in the quiet North Wales town of Mold. Had I realized then that the musical box was indeed a time machine I would have asked my grandmother for it, she would have kept it for me, and it would be on my desk now.

*

Now, here's a curious fact about travelling back in time: philosophers like to illustrate its difficulties, and perhaps its impossibility, by considering the case of an imaginary time traveller who kills off one of his or her grandparents at such an early age as to preclude his own birth and thus his dreadful deed. The fascination of this traditional vein of logical argument obscures an underlying fantasy, unthinkable not only in its paradoxicality but ethically, comprising as it does both murder and an esoteric form of suicide. Among our eminent contemporaries who have scratched their heads over the paradox, Professor Hugh Mellor of Cambridge has a version that targets the grandfather, while Professor Michael Lockwood of Oxford opts for the grandmother. But if I could meet my grandparents again, far from shortening their lives I would expend a little of my own in trying to salvage at least a memory of theirs. How little I know of them! What was their background? I remember my grandmother shortly before she died telling me that her grandfather once ate his dinner off the face of the clock on the Liver Building in Liverpool. My parents dismissed this as the ramblings of old age when I reported it to them, but I take it as truth and like to think that this great-great-grandfather of mine was a city dignitary who partook of a banquet for which the clock face served as a table, before its installation marked the completion of Liverpool's temple of mercantilism. No doubt the mayor or some such grandee sat at the head of the table, that is, at twelve o'clock. What o'clock, what potential now, did my grandmother's grandfather represent? But I know nothing about this almost fabulous ancestor, and indeed my memories of my grandparents themselves are hardly more than textural. When I ride back in time – on the musical box perhaps – to Mold (the very name recaptures the little town as it was when my parents used to bring me there on occasional holiday visits almost a lifetime ago), I encounter on the staircase behind the shop the soft indulgent bulk of my grandmother, and glimpse my tall, rigid grandfather, ignoring me out of shyness rather than antipathy, turning away in the doorspace of a further room. Now that I am old enough to be the grandfather of the child I then was, I can understand something of the distance he chose to occupy, but I cannot communicate this fellow feeling, for that was then, as they say, and this is now.

*

Now and again I used to lose myself in two paintings that hung on that staircase: *La Rixe* (the brawl) by Meissonier, Queen Victoria's favourite painter, and Millet's *Angelus*, so much admired by Salvador Dali. Both represent instants of stasis. In the first, a pack of cards lies scattered on the floor among overturned table, chairs and wine bottles; two gamblers have leaped to confront each other and are being restrained by their companions. One of the antagonists has a dagger; a man behind him tries to twist it out of his grasp while another seizes him around the chest. (It can hardly have been my gentle grandmother who told me that the model for the man with the dagger is said to have died of his frustrated exertions in this role.) The other would-be fighter is trying to draw his sword but is obstructed by a fifth man, who holds him back with one arm and stretches out the other towards the face of the man with the dagger, hand wide open and fingers crooked, in a gesture that shouts 'No!' so loudly that time is stopped. Every detail of the scene is meticulously rendered, though one could scarcely call the result lifelike. Meissonier masters time, and here a moment is preserved as if under brown varnish, but space is beyond him. As one critic has written, 'his prodigious power of decomposition left him incapable of putting anything together again'. And in this painting the dimension of depth is slightly awry and distances have been misjudged, so that figures seem to step through each other. (But perhaps this unshapely space is masterly, Einsteinian, a General Relativity of drunken rage.) The other painting, in contrast, offers contemplative stillness. The chimes of the Angelus, conducted by a flock of rooks high in the evening sky, come from a church tower on the horizon of an endless plain, to two potato-pickers. The young couple stand with bowed heads, at their feet a half-filled basket. They are statuesque figures, alone in the vast emptiness. In one of his homages to this painting Dali transforms them into rook-haunted ruinous towers much taller than the funereal cypresses growing around their bases. Dali, with his X-ray eyes, also made out that Millet has painted the potato basket over the representation of a coffin, in which, perhaps, the two peasants had brought their dead child for burial. In another interpretation of the scene Dali diagnoses sexual tension; he depicts the moment after that of the Angelus, in which the male peasant leaps at the female as urgently as Meissonier's furious gamesters strain to stab each other. Of course as a child I was aware of none of these hypothetical histories. For me each of the two paintings in the staircase was a banner parading through all time an ancient and incomprehensible Now.

*

Nowadays analytic philosophers such as the professors mentioned above are not professionally interested in the phenomenology and, even less, the poetics of time, neither as evoked by Proust's soggy cake-crumbs nor as measured by Dali's melting watches. Both of them pay more attention to the dry argumentation of the Cambridge philosopher John McTaggart, who in 1908 published a paper on 'The Unreality of Time'. There are, says McTaggart, two ways of describing time. One of them seems to fit our experience of time's flow; it uses such terms as past, present and future, tomorrow, a long time ago, and so on, all anchored in the concept of the present moment, the Now. (Today's philosophers would call this version 'tensed time'.) An event may at some time be future, then be present, and finally be past. (I can say an event 'is future', as shorthand for 'will take place in the future'; the details of English tense grammar don't enter into this discussion.) But how can an event have these contradictory qualities, of being future, present, and past? Because of course it has them at different times, we rush in to say! Thus it might be that in the past it was future, at present it is present, and in the future it will be past. But this will not do, responds McTaggart; it seeks to explicate past, present and future in terms of past, present and future, and so leads us up the garden path into vicious circles. Therefore tensed time does not exist. 'Nonsense!' cries Professor Mellor (and I have seen him denounce nonsense, in a seminar on metaphysics I crept into once: a fierce, compact personage, he turns his back on the source of nonsense and curls up in his chair as if shielding himself from contamination, while his errant post-graduate students bite their lips). Future, present and past, he says, are not qualities of events, they are relationships. To remark that an event is future is to say that it takes place after the making of the remark. Thus the terminology of tensed time depends on that of tenseless time, time as ordered by the relationships 'before', 'simultaneous with', and 'after', and specified by dates such as 1066 or phrases like 'just before breakfast on Tim Robinson's fifth Christmas Day'. But this apparently objective version of time runs into difficulties too, at least in the outer reaches of modern physics. Before Einstein it could be supposed that any two observers would in principle agree as to which of two events happened first; but Special Relativity says that they may not, if they are in motion relative to each other. Indeed, as Einstein's great master Hermann Minkowski said in 1908, 'Henceforth space by itself, and time by itself, are doomed to fade away into mere shadows, and only a kind of union of the two will preserve an independent reality.' Since then spacetime itself has been proved to be warped, to be expanding, probably to have a beginning and perhaps an end, to contain holes, to be stuffed with six or seven other dimensions tightly curled up like subatomic horsehair. This welter of wonders entails impenetrable complications for the theory of time, seeming to imply that the concepts of past, present and future have at the most a local and almost a person-specific degree of adequacy. Professor Lockwood's book on the subject is admirably lucid, but its title gives due warning: *The labyrinth of time*. I used to think I comprehended these matters, but I am not so sure of my grip on time as of now.

*

Now, or never, having awoken my grandparent's old house from the comfortable doze it has enjoyed in my memory for so long, is the time to record another aspect of it, before the mice of forgetfulness gnaw it all away. Behind the front ground-floor room occupied by the shop, down a few stairs, was a semi-basement – a mere coal-hole, I suppose, but it seemed spacious to me – into which coke used to be avalanched every now and then through a hatch in the rear wall of the house. I liked to stand on a wooden step by the coke-hill and look out of this hatch, my chin on a level with the cobbles of the back lane.

Opposite, the sooty-stoned parish church towered among tall trees. The shadowy space between the backs of the houses and the churchyard wall was projected into the unreal by my worm's-eye perspective on it. When, just now, I summoned up maps and photographs from the internet I found that this little region of mystery no longer exists; the back lane and the terrace houses of which my grandparents' was one have been swept away and replaced by a sloping lawn, a bland civic amenity offering a view of the old church from the main street. The lane mattered to me because it led to a children's playground with a few swings, a small roundabout, and a pair of parallel bars. As a devotee of Tarzan I was proud of my ability to hang by my knees from one of these bars. My head must have been close to the ground in this position, for once when my long-suffering knees relaxed their grip I came down with a thump that sent me wailing back along the lane, but did no visible damage to my skull. (I could say that I have never been the same since, but that is true of every moment of my life.) My image of myself upside-down, bat-like, in the rectangular space below the bar, like that of myself at the hatch with my chin on its sill, gives me a measure of my size at that time of my life. Our subjective experience of the flow of time, says Hugh Mellor, is no evidence that time really does flow; what we actually experience is change in ourselves, the accumulation of memories, of memories of memories. This must include memories of stages in physical growth, and of the incidents that knock such memories into our heads. My brief surrender to gravity, my tearful return down the lane, are lodged in the loops of my brain-stuff, as are my grandfather quelling my sobs with the testy formula, 'Now then!' and my grandmother applying as a verbal salve to my sore head a soft dove-like repetition of 'Now, now . . .'

*

Now, and to end, let me open what always felt to me to be the secret heart of my grandparents' house. At floor-level in a corner of the sitting room was a cupboard full of games that must have been old-fashioned even in those days of my childhood. Sometimes I would delve into it before breakfast, when there was a faint acrid tang of dead ashes in the room, as yet unvisited by the day's routines. There were tiddlywinks and marbles, packs of cards for playing Happy Families, and shallow boxes that opened up into trays scattered with cardboard fish one could angle for with a little magnet on a string. On the floor of the cupboard, or between the leaves of big illustrated books, I used occasionally to find more valuable fish too, escaped perhaps from a long-lost pouch; they were delicately cut out from wafers of mother-of-pearl, and must have been tokens in an antique parlour game, as I realized much later when I read in a Jane Austen novel of a young lady who after an evening visit could talk of nothing but the fish she had won and the fish she had lost. Most precious of all was a set of ivory spillikins in a narrow little box, also of ivory, with a delicately fretted lid. Each spillikin had a slender stem some five inches long, and a head representing a Chinese sage, a sickle moon, a long-tailed bird or some fabulous species of animal. Piled on a tabletop, they formed a tangle from which with the aid of a little hook one tried to extricate one spillikin at a time without causing the least trembling amongst the rest, an operation as delicate as that of capturing an elusive memory without awakening others interlinked with it that one would rather leave undisturbed. Where is this test of the subtle and steady hand now? At the bottom of a box of crumpled letters, photographs and ephemera, perhaps, forgotten in the attic of some house I have long quitted. And the moment of first finding them, in my grandparents' cupboard? All events have equal claims to a tenseless reality, says Professor Mellor; all have their address in spacetime. Among them must be the contents of everyone's Nows, whether past, present or future, remembered or forgotten, observed or unobserved. While it is not quite pleasing to hear that countless redundant trivialities are of the stuff of the universe, I like to think that the particular Nows that have been picked out by our passionate attention to them are stacked away separately, as it were in vaults, like paintings bought by a millionaire on the advice of experts. If connoisseurship of memory is the human role in this indiscriminately memorious world, then among those treasures is certainly my grandmother's quietly challenging utterance on first emptying out the box of spillikins for me: 'Now!'

The Tower of Silence

We said goodbye at the gate.
His first step took him over the horizon.
We stood around his parting footprint.
'He must be taller than we thought,' we said.

We met him near the West Hampstead tube station: a young man we knew little of beyond the fact that he, like us, lived in a nearby house that was awaiting demolition. He had a small bag slung over one shoulder. 'Where are you off to?' we asked. 'Kathmandu,' he replied, and strode onwards.

That evening I mentioned him to Anna, founder of the local self-help organization that had argued the Council into letting some of its stock of unoccupied housing be used temporarily by such indefinables as ourselves and the Kathmandu pilgrim. She had not known of his departure; but we were all as elusive as eels, and she was unsurprised. The next day she went to the house to see if it was suitable for others of her houseless clients. 'He's left a few old books you might be interested in,' she said to me later; 'and the house itself is worth seeing.'

Lured by the whiff of old books, I hurried round there myself. The house, Victorian, detached, three stories and attic over a semi-basement, stood in a tangle of scrawny buddleia bushes. The back door to the basement flat gave at my push. I stepped in, and stood amazed. The ceiling of the flat's main room together with the floors and ceilings of the room above it, and of the one above that, and the one above that, had been removed. The departed resident must have started in the attic by prizing up the floorboards and sawing through the joists beneath them, and so on down from floor to floor. I saw no sign of the piles of timber this operation must have produced; perhaps they had been sold to fund his travels. One wall of the great empty tower had a door in it at each level, all hanging open; another wall had four tiled fireplaces one high above another. Craning my neck I could make out some flowers, still fresh-looking, in a jam jar on the topmost mantelpiece.

After some rooting around in cupboards and cardboard boxes I found the books. They were mouldy and battered, but a nineteenth-century guide to Wales with engravings of famous views was worth salvaging. Then a ragged volume with the title *Sahara*, or perhaps *Saraha*, caught my eye. It seemed to be the work of a Buddhist sage of some such name. I dipped into the long and scholarly introduction, and flipped through the many detailed notes at the end of the book. Intrigued, I eagerly turned to the text itself, only to find that it had been ripped out. What I had in my hand was the husk, academic analysis and pedantic commentary; the precious kernel, the divine message, was gone – to Kathmandu, no doubt.

The Tower of Silence always stands in a city somewhere. No street-noise reaches its summit. With every dawn it gives itself a new horizon. The doorman is polite but remote.

One day when the Tower was in Istanbul I stepped out of it into what had been the courtyard of a Venetian caravanserai. The domes of the arcade had long fallen in. Squatting below the ragged circles of sky were women, their hands busy picking rags to bits, sorting short lengths of thread by colour. In Terre Haute, Indiana, right opposite the doorway of the Tower, were the boarded-up windows of an apartment once used by the prostitute Al Capone blamed for his gonorrhoea and sent one of his gang to murder. In Paris when I went to cross the road from the Tower's splendid porte-cochère I had to step around two weeping women locked in each other's arms. They had just come out of the Institute Curie's radiotherapy centre, having, I surmised, just received the results of tests; the younger woman had burst into tears as soon as they were free of the Institute's constraining orderliness, and the elder, her mother perhaps, was comforting her. In Dubrovnik the Tower's lobby formed part of the promenade around the city walls and faced the back of the jail. Something small was hanging on a string from the bars of a little window: a Turkish cigarette package, ten Bafras, blue, empty. A vortex of traffic separated the Tower's front steps from the blood-cemented stones of the Coliseum in Rome. There were so many people crossing the street on which the Tower stood in the city of London that some of them had to step over the little drunken Scotsman lying on his back agitating his limbs like a capsized beetle. The Lion Dance went round and round the Tower in Bangkok; the six capering monkeys, their masks lumpy coagulations of spite, harried the exhausted lion, which feebly snapped its huge jaws at them. The child who slept among the Tower's dustbins in Calcutta had dragons of pleated paper for sale; he could make one of them run up onto the back of another as if in copulation. His mother in Dublin sat against one of the Tower's plant containers all day and apparently owned nothing but a plastic cup. When the Tower returned to Istanbul there was a man living in the concrete-pillared parking space under it. The bottom half of his body had been replaced by a curved piece of rubber cut from a tyre, and he swung himself along by means of two weights in his hands. As I watched he levered himself off a step onto a lower one, bounced and fell over with a curse. Two other men lurking in the darkness further back laughed at him. And so on, world without end.

Contrescarpe

Albertine, of 'Hispano-Sarrasin blood', born and abandoned 1937, Algiers; adopted by a French family and taken to Aix-en-Provence; raped by her adoptive uncle, arrested for '*vagabondage*', placed by the family in a reformatory; escaped to Paris, lived by theft and prostitution; visited her adoptive father and stole his pistol; arrested in the course of armed robbery, sent to Fresnes Prison; showed herself to be a gifted student but a recalcitrant prisoner with an unquenchable resentment of authority; escaped at night by jumping from a high wall, breaking her ankle bone or *astragale*, crawled half-naked and in agony to the nearby highway, was scooped up by a motorcyclist: *An arm encircled my shoulders, another slipped under my knees; I was lifted, carried off: he carried me securely and gently. I had left the mud and I walked, in his arms, between heaven and earth*. Her savior Julien Sarrazin, born 1924, Feuquières, near Amiens, seventh of his violent, alcoholic criminal father's twelve children; the family's main food-gatherer during the Occupation, arrested 1943 with his younger brother George for robbing trains bound for Germany; condemned to fifteen years' hard labour, participated in the prison revolt of Melun in 1944 and tried to escape with George, who was shot dead by the Germans. Recaptured, released in 1953; continued to live by crime; found Albertine, hid her in his mother's house; both of them repeatedly drawn to crime, and it was in jail that they married and Albertine wrote the autobiographical novel, *L'Astragale* (1965), that made her famous and notorious. At the end of her book, shortly after Julien has been released from prison Albertine is rearrested. She accepts her fate with a smile: *We will meet again on the luminous platform. Once more, one of us is at the foot of the slope. Turn by turn we must clamber and haul*. And it seems they did attain to that sunlit height. A grateful former client of

Albertine's bought them an old farm near Montpellier. Photographs from this last period show her delicate but rebellious little face and Julien's tender watch over her; the impression is of a golden time, but it was brief. Her health was ruinous and in 1967, aged 29, she died from a botched kidney operation; Julien pursued those responsible through the legal system, and after many setbacks saw them condemned to short prison terms and was awarded damages of 40,000 francs as what the judge termed 'exact reparation for the loss of his wife'.

*

In 2011 M and I stayed for some months in the Centre Culturel lrlandais in Paris, near Place de la Contrescarpe, which I passed through almost every day. The name interested me, and when I found a grubby old paperback of that title in one of the heaped trays outside a bookshop in the Rue des Écoles, I snatched it up. To my surprise it turned out to be the autobiography of Julien Sarrazin, and it is a vigorous, slangy, passionate work, a worthy response to *L'Astragale*, which Albertine called her 'little love-story for Julien'. It ends with his finding of the girl dropped out of the sky: *After that my sole concern was to hide and care for the kid. Her injury was very serious, nursing took up months and months, but I had found a reason for living, a precious and savage reason. I felt myself responsible, without analysis. What ought to be done, must be done.*

Contrescarpe appeared in 1974 and is long out of print. The word does not occur in Julien's book, I found, but an introductory note mentions this mysterious title and suggests that it is easier to fall down the *contrescarpe* of life than to climb up it. An archaeologist friend met in Paris told me that it is a term of fortification: the inner wall or slope of a defensive ditch is the *escarpe* and the outer one the *contrescarpe*. He also pointed out a plaque in the Rue Descartes, which slopes down northwards from Place de la Contrescarpe, indicating the position of a long-vanished gate of the wall built by Philip II Augustus in 1200–1215 to protect the city against the Anglo-Norman Plantagenets while he was away on the Third Crusade. In the fourteenth century this wall was strengthened by digging a large ditch in front of it and heaping the spoil against the inside of the wall. Craggy lengths and cross-sections of the wall show up here and there among the smooth-plastered facades lining Rue Descartes, but the ditch and its outer slope that gave the little square its name have long been levelled out of existence.

In 1955 the psychogeographer Guy Debord, who was shortly to found the Situationist International, wrote: *It has long been said that the desert is monotheistic. Is it illogical or devoid of interest to observe that the district in Paris between Place de la Contrescarpe and Rue de l'Arbalète conduces rather to atheism, to oblivion and to the disorientation of habitual reflexes?* One can only answer such a query by imagined revisitings. Place de la Contrescarpe is small and frequently crowded. On three of its sides are restaurants and bars fronted by ranks of chairs and tables on the pavements, under red canopies. The centre of the Place is marked by a little fountain surrounded by a rather sparse grove of young trees, within a circle of cast iron posts linked by loops of chain. The space immediately within the chained circle is the preserve of two street-dwellers, stubby men wearing layers of clothing made grey by weather. One of them has his hair in dreadlocks. They lie stretched out on bits of cardboard, or on the bare cobbles. Occasionally they exchange a few brief curses but otherwise seem to have little to do with each other. My passing glimpses of their tedious and comfortless existences tell me little about how they live, where they find food, where they spend their nights. It does not seem that God tempers the wind to them. There is also an elderly lady in a long greyish overcoat who circulates in the square accosting passers-by. Her speech is a shouted whisper like a sudden venting of compressed air. Once she materialized unnoticed behind M and addressed her with an explosive hiss of 'Madame!' that frightened her into jumping from one side of me to the other as if fleeing a curse – a most unhabitual reflex for her, normally so open-hearted.

Five narrow streets diverge from the Place, two of them climbing northwards and westwards, two falling eastwards towards the Jardin des Plantes, and the other, Rue Mouffetard, dropping steeply away to the south. This street is the spine of the area indicated by Debord. It is narrow, cobbled and picturesque, but not too self-consciously so. There are queues outside certain pâtisseries, dashing young men preside over smoking hotplates in crêperies no bigger than cupboards, the jewellers' displays and vegetable stalls are exquisitely colour-coordinated, scores of identical cane chairs press together as closely as possible outside restaurants around corners off the street. In the Christmas season a web of countless tiny lights that might have been scissored out of the Milky Way is suspended above the street from end to end. Among the branches of the trees in the Place more lights cleverly imitate the soft fall of big snowflakes. Everything is enchanted; even one of the street-dwellers lying by the fountain as if fallen to the very foot of the contrescarpe of life, oblivious to the busy shoppers stepping around and over him, is parcelled up in silver foil, a Christmas present that nobody wants.

List of images

p. 24   Wool gathering, Aughrus Beg, May 2013

p. 33   0 m., Cartoor Beg, summer 2005

p. 35   Déjà vu, The Sky Road, March 2012

p. 36   Pearse's cottage, Ros Muc, September 2011

p. 37   Phototaxis, Beaghcauneen, March 2014

p. 38   Unfolding Roundstone I, Roundstone, September 2011

p. 39   Unfolding Roundstone II, Roundstone, June 2012

p. 40   Mám Éan, the pass of birds, Mám Éan, December 2010

p. 41   Still tracing, *Connemara: a one-inch map, with introduction and gazetteer*

p. 43   'usque ad ultimum terrae, ubi nunc paruitas mea esse uidetur inter alienigenas', *Confessio* 1, Saint Patrick, Mám Éan, December 2010

p. 44   *Listening to the wind*, last page, and *Map*, Dublin, March 2014

p. 45   Out of field, Na Siáin / the fairy hills, Sheeauns, April 2011

p. 46   Folding landscape, Errisbeg, April 2011

p. 48   Forest tree, 4014 B.C., Bunowen, April 2011

p. 49   Photogenic drawing, Lough Fee, Letterettrin, April 2011

p. 50   [left] Quay at the beach of the women, Gorteennaglogh, March 2012

p. 50   [right] Quay at the beach of the women, *Connemara: a one-inch map, with introduction and gazetteer*

p. 53   Refloating Inishbofin, Aughrus Beg, May 2012

p. 55   Derryclare Island, N59, October 2012

p. 57   Blotched, Claddaghduff, August 2012

p. 58   Erosion, Cartoor Beg, summer 2006

p. 59   Trá na nÉan, the beach of the birds, Gooreen, August 2011

p. 61   Faul / the fences, Faul, April 2011

p. 62   Nymphaea alba, Roundstone Bog, July 2010

p. 64   Last pool of darkness, Rosroe, winter 2004

p. 65   For the birds, Rosroe, March 2014

p. 66   Claddaghduff / black shore, Claddaghduff, summer 2006

p. 67   White noise: an outcry inarticulate, Omey Strand, May 2012

p. 68   *A little Gaelic kingdom*, 250, Nérac, France, April 2013

p. 69   Breaker, Gooreen, summer 2005

p. 70   Details, *Connemara: a one-inch map, with introduction and gazetteer*

p. 71   Detail, *Connemara: a one-inch map, with introduction and gazetteer*

p. 73   *Verity*'s anchor, Aughrus Beg, August 2013

p. 74   The boneyard in the mist, Moorneen, April 2011

p. 75   Letterfrack Industrial School for Boys burial ground, Letterfrack, August 2012

p. 76   Children's Burial Ground, Rusheenduff, May 2013

p. 77   The depth of field, Cartoor Beg, May 2013

p. 78   [left] Detail, *Connemara: a one-inch map, with introduction and gazetteer*

p. 78   [right] Dresser, Halfmace, April 2012

p. 79   [left] Dislocation, Letternoosh, April 2012

p. 79   [right] Detail, *Connemara: a one-inch map, with introduction and gazetteer*

p. 80   Bullish diptych I, Cathair an Dúin / the fort of the bluff, Curragh, May 2013

p. 81   Bullish diptych II, Cathair an Dúin / the fort of the bluff, Curragh, May 2013

p. 82   Galvanized, Curragh, May 2013

p. 84   Walking the horizon, Letternoosh, May 2013

p. 85   [left] Puzzled S, Gooreen, summer 1999

p. 85   [right] Northside Carna, Carna, August 2013

p. 86   Féichín's well, Gooreen, April 2011

p. 87   [left] Watching High, Gooreenatinny, spring 2000

p. 87   [right] Washed-up, Trá Rabhach, Gooreenatinny, June 2010

p. 88   [left] H and per se and S I, Rossadillisk, 9 April 2012

p. 88   [middle] H and per se and S II, Gooreen, summer 2004

p. 88   [right] H and per se and S III, Rossadillisk, 9 April 2012

p. 89   Mermaid's hair at Béal an Oileáin / the mouth of the island, Gooreen, May 2013

p. 90   *The Irish Times*, Saturday, July 30th, 2005, at Féar Milis / sweet grass, Friday, June 1st, 2012, 19:38'46", Mannin More, July 2012

p. 91   Seanadh Chiamhair / the gloomy slope, Shanakeever, April 2011

p. 92   Sensitive surface, Gooreen, May 2013

p. 93   Trá Mhíl / whale beach, Dolan, March 2012

p. 94   The patches / na Paistí, Patches, May 2012

p. 96   Still surface, Derryclare, August 2011

p. 97   Still pane, Aughrus Beg, August 2012

p. 99   [left] Omey Strand Quotation I, Omey Strand, spring 2000

p. 99   [right] Omey Strand Quotation II, place unknown, spring 2004

p. 101   Sleeping beauty, Arkeen More, June 2012

p. 102   Origin of species, Gooreen, March 2010

p. 104   The depth of the surface, Lotaí, April 2012

p. 105   [left] Plane surface, Omey Island, April 2011

p. 105   [right] The fractals that pass…over there…over there…, Claddaghduff, summer 2006

p. 106   Echolalia, Roundstone Bog, summer 2010

p. 107   The print of nature, Blaceret, France, date unknown

p. 108   At home I, *The last pool of darkness*, 215, home, August 2013

p. 109   [left] At home II, 'Hexagon', home, May 2013

p. 109   [right] At home III, Hexagon, Cartoor Beg, summer 2006

p. 111   Lettergesh East –West, Lettergesh East, April 2011

p. 112   An Gearrán Bán / the white gelding, Garraunbaun, January 2012

p. 113   Bog-cottons, Lough Inagh Valley, summer 1999

p. 115   [left] Stranded hedgehog, Gooreen, July 2010

p. 115   [right] Horse point/ Aughrus beg, Aughrus Beg, September 2011

p. 117   H, sweet grass at Féar Milis, Mannin More, June 2012

p. 118   [I] Barbarus hic ego sum, R340, April 2011

p. 119   [II] qui non intellegor ulli, Ovid, *Tristia* V, x, 37, Teernakill South, R336, April 2011

p. 121   A stranded sperm whale on Trá Chóil, Omey Island, photographed at low tide, just after dawn, Cloon, January 2012

p. 123   Nowhere now here, Roundstone, April 2011

p. 125   A land without shortcuts, Emlagh, summer 2006

Works cited

Debord, G. 1955 Introduction à une critique de la géographie urbaine. *Les Lèvres Nues* **6**.

Eliot, T.S. 1920 *Ara Vos Prec.* **London. Ovid Press.**

Flowers, F.A. (ed.) 1999 *Portraits of Wittgenstein*, Vol. 4. Bristol. Thoemmes Continuum.

Freud, S. 1913 *The interpretation of dreams.* A.A. Brill (trans.). New York. The Macmillan Company.

Gette, P.-A. 2011 *Des cheveux de Vénus aux splendeurs de la nuit: Proposition transectale de Digne à Auzet & vice versa.* Crisnée, Belgium. Yellow Now.

Gette, P.-A. 1977 *De quelques lisières. Prolégomènes à un essai de définition de la notion d'écotone.* Paris. Cheval d'Attaque.

Hazlitt, W. 1825 Mr. Wordsworth. *The spirit of the age: or contemporary portraits*, 231–50. London. Henry Colburn.

Heaney, S. (ed.) 1988 *The essential Wordsworth.* New York. Ecco Press.

Lockwood, M. 2005 *The labyrinth of time.* Oxford University Press.

Mac Giollarnáth, S. 1949 *Mo dhúthaigh fhiáin.* Baile Átha Cliath. Brún agus Ó Nualláin.

Macfarlane, R. 2011 Perspectives on Connemara. Film. Cambridge, May 2011. Available at https://humanities.exeter.ac.uk/english/research/projects/aarp/timrobinson/ (last accessed May 2013).

Mandelbrot, B. 1967 How long is the coast of Britain? *Science* **156**.

Mandelbrot, B. 1980 Fractal aspects of the iteration of $z \rightarrow \lambda z (1-z)$ for complex λ and z. *Annals of the New York Academy of Science* **357**, 249–59.

Mc Carthy, P. (trans.) 2011 *My name is Patrick: St Patrick's Confessio.* Dublin. Royal Irish Academy.

McTaggart, J.M.E. 1908 The unreality of time. *Mind: A Quarterly Review of Psychology and Philosophy* **17**, 456-473.

Mellor, D.H. 1998 *Real time II.* London. Routledge.

Minkowski, H. 1952 Space and Time. In H.A. Lorentz, A. Einstein, H. Minkowski and H. Weyl, *The principle of relativity: a collection of original memoirs on the Special and General Theory of Relativity* (address to the 80th Assembly of German Natural Scientists and Physicians on September 21, 1908), 75–91. New York. Dover.

Murphy, R. 2013 *Poems 1952–2012.* Dublin. The Lilliput Press.

Ovid 1939 *Tristia. Ex Ponto.* A.L. Wheeler (trans.). Loeb Classical Library, Cambridge, MA. Harvard University Press.

Robinson, T. 1985 *Mapping south Connemara: Parts 1–29: Cashel, Carna, Cill Chiaráin. Roundstone.* Folding Landscapes.

Robinson, T. 1986 *Stones of Aran: pilgrimage.* Dublin. The Lilliput Press Ltd.

Robinson, T. 1990 *Connemara: Part 1: introduction and gazetteer; Part 2: a one-inch map.* Roundstone. Folding Landscapes.

Robinson, T. 1995 *Stones of Aran: Part 2: labyrinth.* Dublin. The Lilliput Press Ltd.

Robinson, T. 1996 *Oileán Árann: a map of the Aran Islands with a companion to the map.* Roundstone. Folding Landscapes.

Robinson, T. 1996 *Setting foot on the shores of Connemara*. Dublin. The Lilliput Press Ltd.

Robinson, T. 1997 *Stones of Aran: Part 2: labyrinth*. London. Penguin.

Robinson, T. 1999 *The Burren: a map of the uplands of north-west County Clare*. Roundstone. Folding Landscapes.

Robinson, T. 2001 *My time in space*. Dublin. The Lilliput Press Ltd.

Robinson, T. 2002 *Tales and imaginings*. Dublin. The Lilliput Press Ltd.

Robinson, T. 2007 *Connemara: listening to the wind*. London. Penguin.

Robinson, T. 2009 *Connemara: the last pool of darkness*. London. Penguin.

Robinson, T. 2012 'A land without shortcuts: in defence of the distinctiveness of places'. *The Dublin Review* 46 (Spring 2012), 25–44.

Robinson, T. 2012 *Connemara: a little Gaelic kingdom*. London. Penguin.

Sarrazin, A. 1965 *L'Astragale*. Paris. Pauvert.

Sarrazin, J. 1974 *Contrescarpe*. Paris. R. Laffont.

Wittgenstein, L. 1958 *Philosophical investigations*. G.E.M. Anscombe (trans.), 2nd edn. Oxford.

Wittgenstein, L. 1961 *Tractatus logico-philosophicus*. D.F. Pears and B.F. McGuinness (trans.). London.